LEAP OF
FAITH

FRANKIE DETTORI

LEAP OF FAITH

with Boris Starling

HarperCollins*Publishers*

HarperCollins*Publishers*
1 London Bridge Street
London SE1 9GF

www.harpercollins.co.uk

HarperCollins*Publishers*
1st Floor, Watermarque Building, Ringsend Road
Dublin 4, Ireland

First published by HarperCollins*Publishers* 2021

1 3 5 7 9 10 8 6 4 2

Quotes on pages 184, 257, 258 and 273
previously published by the *Guardian*.

A catalogue record of this book is
available from the British Library

HB ISBN 978-0-00-846546-9
TPB ISBN 978-0-00-846547-6

Printed and bound in the UK using 100%
renewable electricity at CPI Group (UK) Ltd

MIX
Paper from
responsible sources
FSC™ C007454

To my amazing family and much love to
Catherine, Leo, Ella, Mia, Tallula and Rocco

CONTENTS

PROLOGUE

Derby Day. There's nothing else like it.

It's our Super Bowl, our Wimbledon, our Monaco Grand Prix. It's the race I dreamed of winning as a young kid on a pony back in Milan. It's the greatest race in the world.

I slept badly, as I always do the night before. There's something almost reassuring about that now: it's how I know I'm up for it. The night I get eight hours' uninterrupted kip before the Derby is the day I hang up my boots for good. I used to shy away from the nerves, but now I'm older and (apparently) wiser, I embrace them: I know they're what I need to help me perform at my best. If I didn't get nervous for this kind of moment, I wouldn't have a soul. I carry that sense of people's expectations: I feel that everything I do today, even the

1

smallest thing, will be under the microscope. It's horrible, but it's great. I wouldn't swap it for the world.

I make my own coffee, as I always do. Espresso: hot, black, strong and Italian.

The kids have made a banner for me. GOOD LUCK, DADDY, it says, draped across the kitchen window. I fight back the tears. It's not just that they're old enough now to know what this means – Leo's 15, Ella's 14, Mia's 12, Tallula's 11 and Rocco's 10 – it's that even by Derby standards, this one promises to be special.

It's the first one I've ridden in four years. For pretty much all my career before that, I rode the Derby every year: 19 out of 20 years, and the one I missed was only because I'd almost been killed in an aircraft crash 10 days before. And then it all went to shit. Out of favour at the stables I'd been with for so long. Suspended for taking cocaine. And then, when I returned, the forgotten man, the ghost of Derbies past who couldn't beg, steal or borrow a mount on the biggest day of all.

Until now.

I kiss the kids goodbye one by one, followed by my wife Catherine. Last year, when things were so bad I considered walking away from the sport altogether, she sat me down and gave it to me straight. 'You keep telling me how fucking good you are,' she said. 'Well, now's the time to show it.'

Now's the time indeed. I hug her hard. She's been there for me through all the ups and downs, and we've had more of both than the Big Dipper on Blackpool Beach. She puts up with my moods and my neuroses. When I say that I couldn't have done any of this without her, I mean it from the bottom of my heart.

I drive the short distance to Newmarket, where the helicopter's waiting. It's less flash than it sounds. A lot of jockeys are based around here, and traffic on a Saturday can be horrendous, so clubbing together for a helicopter ride is a no-brainer. It's 40 minutes or so to Epsom, and the journey passes largely in silence. There's usually a lot of chat between jockeys – we spend so long together and know each other so well that the banter and in-jokes come thick and fast – but today everyone prefers to be alone with their thoughts. I look out of the window at the great sprawl of London below and count the racecourses I can see, the places I know like the back of my hand and which have seen so many of my triumphs and disasters. Ascot, Kempton Park, Sandown and Windsor in the distance out west; Lingfield, Brighton and Goodwood up ahead to the south.

Almost before I know it, we're here. Out of the helicopter and into the special hum of Epsom at its finest.

I'm riding Golden Horn today, so I look for his trainer, John Gosden. It's not long before I see him, but then again it's not hard to spot someone who's 6-foot-5 and wears the most distinctive fedora in racing.

If it weren't for John, I wouldn't be here. This is the second time in my career he's backed me when no one else would, and I'm determined to repay his faith. We might appear an odd couple – he's 20 years older and a foot taller than me for starters, and he's old-school British ice cool whereas I'm Italian fire – but he totally gets me and understands me. There are few trainers as good as him – and even fewer human beings. I love working with him. We're as happy as a pair of old lags doing one last job together.

'Come on,' he says. 'Let's walk the course.'

I do this every Derby Day. It's partly to get a sense of how firm the ground is, as every horse has its preferred conditions and you have to adjust your race tactics accordingly. It's partly tradition and routine: I've done it so often now that I'd feel unsettled if I didn't. And it's partly to soak up the atmosphere, which even a few hours before the big race of the afternoon is already buzzing. I see the funfair, smell barbecues, hear the sizzle of meat and the happy chatter. People cheer when they see me. A chant goes up: 'Fran-kie! Fran-kie! Fran-kie!' I smile, wave at them, perform a mock bow. John smiles. He's seen it all before. He knows how much of a show-man I am – it's racing, it's entertainment, so why shouldn't I be? – but he knows too that for me being a jockey comes first and last. To the public, I'm Frankie. On the race card and on my racing breeches, I'm L. Dettori: L for Lanfranco and, if I win this, L for Lazarus too. Frankie's the showman; L. Dettori's the jockey. Two parts of a whole.

The course is a mile and a half long, so it takes us about half an hour to walk it. It's one of the most testing flat-racing tracks on the planet, not least because in the first half mile it rises 150 feet, almost the height of Nelson's Column. From the stalls at the start, it's like looking up a mountain. You can't win the race in that first half mile, but you can definitely lose it. I know not to go out too fast or be too far back; I know not to be stuck behind a bad horse or boxed in on the rails. I also know that Golden Horn's the favourite, and he's so strong that all I need to do is keep out of trouble and let him do the rest. The ground is good, firm in parts: perfect for him to show his pace.

The track flattens off at the mile post before starting to go downhill. The climb will take a lot out of Golden Horn, so this is where I'll get him to relax, get his breath back, let him freewheel a bit and fill those massive lungs full of oxygen, because then the track starts to descend into Tattenham Corner and the horses begin to speed up again. It's easy to get there too quickly and just as easy to sit too long. Some horses find that their legs can't keep up with it and they start dropping back: downhill into a left turn is trickier than it looks on TV, especially when there are a dozen horses all going for more or less the same piece of turf. I remember the words of Lester Piggott, maybe the greatest of them all, to me many years ago: 'If you're out of position going down the hill, don't try to make up ground. Wait for the straight.' Because in that home straight is where it all plays out, where you find out whether you and the horse have it or you don't. What you can't do on the straight is get trapped on the inside: the track is cambered from right to left, so when horses start to tire they move across and down the hill towards the running rail.

We walk past the three furlong marker. I look at John. He shakes his head. 'Not here,' he says. He indicates the two furlong marker up ahead. 'There. Don't press the button till two out.'

'Exactly my thoughts,' I say. Three out might be too far. But from two out, if Golden Horn goes the way I know he can then even a brick wall won't stop him.

There are seven races here today, and the Derby, which goes off at 4.30 p.m., is the fifth. Even for the biggest race of all, you rarely, if ever, get to have just that and no others. Today I'm lucky: I've only got one other ride, the Investec Private Banking Handicap at 2 p.m., in which I finish fourth on Dutch Uncle. Then I can just relax – *try* to relax – in the weighing room. I watch the other races on TV: William Buick winning on Buratino, Pat Dobbs on Pether's Moon, and Martin Lane on Desert Law. The clock hands crawl, race, crawl again.

Now, finally, it's time.

I put on the silks of Anthony Oppenheimer, Golden Horn's owner: white and black halves, red cap. Very simple, very striking. We go out to the parade ring, where the lads are leading the horses round for the spectators. No matter how many times I've been in a parade ring, and that's literally tens of thousands, the sight of thoroughbreds at their peak always makes me catch my breath. The way their coats gleam, the criss-crossing of veins beneath the skin, the muscles rippling as they walk: it's one of the most beautiful sights on God's earth.

John gives me a leg-up onto Golden Horn. Instantly I try to sense how he's feeling (the horse, not the trainer!) and let him know in return how I am. My mood comes down to him through the reins and the saddle: the way I sit, the way I hold him. *Here we are*, I say to him. *We're the best in the field. Run like you can and no one else can touch you. I believe in you.*

Golden Horn's alert, energised, engaged. I smile. Some horses can be detached and not really there, others can get too excited or overwhelmed by the occasion and are spent before the race even begins. Golden Horn's in that sweet spot between the two. My job is to keep him there.

We leave the ring and go onto the course, past the finish line and canter all the way up to the start. The noise is deafening, and yet I know it's only a fraction of what it will be in a few minutes' time when we come back down here for real. The stands on the outside of the home straight are heaving – packed, solid walls of humanity – and inside the rails spectators are packed ten deep all the way, not just along the straight but round Tattenham and up the hill too.

'Go, Frankie! You can do it, Frankie!'

This time I don't acknowledge them. I'm in the zone now: just me, my horse and the race we're going to run.

The race we're going to win.

Flashes of colour in my vision, the brightness of my rivals' silks: deep blue and orange; pink, white and green; yellow, red and black. Burgundy caps, red caps, black caps. I don't give them more than a glance. It's tempting to try to get a look at who's playing up and who's not, but at this stage that's not going to do much good. I'll see how the others are running in the race itself. Until then it's just noise.

The handlers ease our horses into the stalls and close the gates behind us. I'm drawn in stall eight, two-thirds of the way to the outside: a good draw, neither too low nor too high.

All the horses are in now. At the very edge of my peripheral vision I can sense Epicuris, drawn right on the inside, playing up. There'll be a second till we're released, maybe two. No more.

I take a deep breath. This is it.

Then the gates open. A dozen of the best three-year-olds in the world lunge forward, and we're off and running to a mighty roar from the crowd.

Showtime.

1

FATHER

My grandfather Mario tells me stories.

Even though I don't understand half of what he's talking about, I'm rapt as I sit and listen to him. There's something about him. Presence, that's it. He's not tall – 5-foot-2, maximum – but he's a man's man: tough, stubborn, hard as nails. His face is weathered from a life spent outside, and scored in the lines on his skin are the trials which life throws at you when you're a Sardinian builder in tough times.

'It was the early 1940s, Lanfranco,' he says. 'I was doing odd building jobs, earning money where I could. Sometimes I went down the mines at Carbonia, which Mussolini himself had opened only a few years before. An entire city built to house the miners and their families. Imagine that! Even the name gives you a clue. Carbonia. Coaltown.

'Then Italy joined the war and Hitler invaded Russia, and soon Sardinia was heaving with German soldiers. At least there was no fighting on the island. I was called up and made to live full-time in barracks, which was a bit of a problem because your *nonna*, your grandmother, lived 30 miles away from the camp. I'd cycle over to see her whenever I could, but the bikes were useless and the tyres worse, so whenever I got a puncture I'd have to mend it with whatever I could, sometimes just stuffing straw inside the rim, and keep on going. But of course that slowed things up, and one day the inevitable happened. I didn't make it back to camp in time one Monday morning, so they put me on a charge and locked me in a cell for a month.'

'Did you stop going to see *Nonna*?'

'Ha! Not a chance. The second time it happened they tied me to a pole in the middle of a courtyard and left me there for several days, maybe a week. There were ants crawling all over my body, making me itch like crazy, but of course my hands were tied so I couldn't scratch them. I shook the pole so hard that I broke it clean in two. Of course, they put me back in the cell to teach me a lesson good and proper.

'But Lanfranco, we Dettoris are resolute in matters of the heart. Once I'd completed my sentence I rushed off to see your *nonna* again, and again I didn't get back in time. This time there was no escaping serious punishment. I was sent to the front at Monte Cassino, south of Rome. This was early in 1944. There was a famous old monastery there which the British and Americans were trying to capture, because it was in a strategically vital position. Four times in four months they attacked before finally breaking through.

'It was a bloodbath. Rain fell for weeks on end, and the only way I managed to keep myself from sinking into the mud at night was by sleeping on a lilo, like I was in some posh swimming pool or something. We were in these trenches, and the first thing I learned was this: if you want to be shot at, put your head above the parapet. You did that, you had about a second until the enemy started firing. So I kept low, and the only injury I got was a small scratch on my arm from a stray bullet.'

Now my father Gianfranco tells me how he came to get started.

'I was working for your grandfather in the building trade. He'd done 20 years' mining before starting his own business, and me and your uncles, we were all involved. I mixed cement, someone else carried the cement, someone got the sand, someone got the bricks. Hard work, mixing cement for 10 hours a day with no reward other than a bowl of pasta with beans, a roof over my head and just enough money to go to the cinema. It wasn't the hard work I minded, it was the feeling that there was more to life than this. I was educated, I'd been to school till I was 16. After months of hard labour, I couldn't see any sort of future. One day I'd just had it up to here with the whole thing. I hurled my bucket and shovel into a well and told Mario, "I'm leaving."'

'What did he say?'

'He yelled that I needn't bother coming back.'

Whoever said the Dettoris are stubborn?

'What did you do?'

'I just about had the price of a ticket for the ferry to the mainland. I headed for Rome and found a job washing plates in a restaurant. Then I moved on to a second restaurant where I lived in the cellar, but one night it poured with rain, the cellar flooded and everything I owned got swept away. I had nothing, but I figured I didn't need anything anyway. All I cared about was chasing girls, smoking cigarettes and exploring life, so I worked like hell to pay for my fun. I switched from washing dishes to selling fruit and veg at a market stall, and one of the other stall holders was a copper who owned three trotting horses.

'Long story short, I looked after these horses for a bit, realised I was quite good at it, realised too that there was no money in trotting horses, so I went to the Capannelle Racecourse, offered my services to the first trainer I met and signed up as an apprentice for five years. I was 18 years old and had never sat on a horse in my life. In the next-door stable was this lunatic race-horse called Prince Paddy. He was so mad that no one dared go near him: the only way his stable lad could even brush his coat safely was with a long-handled broom.

'Then that stable lad got the flu and everyone was too scared to fill in for him, so I did it. I was young, fearless, and this was my chance to show people what I could do. So not only did I start looking after Prince Paddy, but I started riding him too. The other lads were prac-tically taking bets as to how long I'd last till he bucked me off. But from the moment I sat on him, it was fine. Maybe he sensed that I was the one person who wasn't scared of him, I don't know. Either way, we hacked round together at a gentle pace as though we'd done it a thousand times before. Next morning, same thing happened. I started riding him out every day, then I got my licence and rode him in my first race. No one gave us a chance, just like no one had given me a chance of staying on him at all, but we won.'

* * *

Dad tells me that as a young jockey he was so disciplined that he was in bed at nine every evening, his jodhpurs laid out nearby without a single crease in them, ready for an early start in the morning. He tells me these things not to show off, but to cement in my brain the lesson he wants me to learn: that life is hard, things can be difficult and anything worth having demands the struggle, the sacrifice and the fight. For years he'd been toiling away in filthy jobs for meagre reward, and unlike a lot of young jockeys with easy money in their pockets, he wasn't in a hurry to throw it all away.

Now he's a champion jockey.

I've never known life with my parents together: their marriage was pretty much over before I was born. They had a whirlwind romance which began when my father visited the Circo Russo travelling circus in Milan, next to the racecourse. Circo Russo wasn't exactly P.T. Barnum: they just about stretched to a pair of camels, a few monkeys, three or four lions and a resident clown. But it was the young girl with long black hair all the way down to her calves who captivated my dad. Trapeze artist, contortionist, juggler, riding on two horses with one leg on each: she did it all. Sitting in the front row, smartly turned out in a suit and tie, with his brand new

Vespa parked outside, my dad couldn't take his eyes off her. Her name was Iris Maria, but everyone called her Mara, and she was only 16. He swept her off her feet, and they were married only a few months later in 1963. It was a grand passion, but it wasn't an easy marriage: my mum had spent her entire life on the move with the circus, like a travelling band of gypsies, and to have that taken away from her and be thrust into a life of domesticity was a huge shock.

Now Dad lives with Christine, whom he met while out riding in Australia just before I was born. Christine has always shared Dad's ambition, enjoys his achievements and does whatever she can to support him, whereas my mother's always hated racing. She just thinks it's stupid and can't begin to understand why and how Dad devoted his life to making horses run as fast as they possibly can. Before I was born he'd often come home full of himself, having won the big race, and she'd reply, 'What race?' Nor did she appreciate the strict disciplines involving my father's weight; he could never be sure his supper would be on the table each evening at 6.30 after a long day's work.

As he became more and more well-known, eventually she was left behind. She loved him for who he was, not for the fact that he was the most famous jockey in Italy. By becoming so successful he needed somebody to take him further, and perhaps my mum wasn't educated enough to take the next step with him. She preferred to retain her simple lifestyle as a housewife to which she had become accustomed and couldn't cope with the fame that came with all his high-profile winners. That's just the way she is.

I've got a sister called Alessandra, though everyone calls her Sandra. She's five years older than me, a lifetime at this age. We live with our mother in Milan. Dad lives no more than half a mile away with Christine, but we don't see too much of him because he's always off riding here, there and everywhere.

I'm five. Dad comes back from England and says he won this race called the 2000 Guineas, and even the name sounds exotic to me. He explains that the guinea was a form of British currency, like the lira but from olden days, and that the race has been run for almost 200 years.

He and Mum sit us down.

'We've discussed it,' my father says. 'Alessandra and Lanfranco, you're coming to live with me and Christine.'

'It's just finances,' my mother says. 'Your father earns more than me, so he's much better placed to look after you and make sure you have a decent start in life. But I want you to know that I'll always be here for you, whatever you need and whenever you need it. All this time you've only been 10 minutes' walk from your dad. Well, now you're just 10 minutes' walk from me.'

'Make your bed.'

  'I hate you.'

  'Clean your teeth.'

  'I hate you.'

  'Have a bath.'

  'I hate you.'

  'Get out of bed.'

  'You can't tell me what to do. You're not my mother!'

Christine and Sandra, going round and round, night after night.

I don't stand up to Christine the way Sandra does, but I think the same way she does.

'Don't talk back to your stepmother like that,' my dad says. 'It's not easy for her, you know. She's strict because she's teaching you the right way. One day you'll see how well she's bringing you up.'

One day, one day. What does he know?

*   *   *

School is school. I don't love it, I don't hate it. It's just there, and like everyone else I enjoy the bits I'm good at and try to ignore the rest. I find maths easy and geography interesting – useful for working out odds and travelling the world – but the other subjects leave me cold. We have an hour and a half for lunch and sport every afternoon, so of course we wolf down the food in five minutes flat and play football for as long as we can. For some reason the school only has basketballs, so that's what we play with. They're so heavy I'm surprised there isn't a broken foot every week. I play up front, the glory position: where else? Centre forward, goal hanger, call it what you want: as long as I'm scoring goals, I don't care.

Sometimes I don't see Dad all week, especially at the height of the season. He's gone before I'm up and back long after I've gone to bed. If he does come back when I'm around he greets me with a smile and a kiss, but then he goes upstairs to change into his shorts, comes back down again, watches the news on television without saying a word, and then retreats behind his newspaper for the rest of the evening as he studies the form for the next afternoon's card.

* * *

Sandra fights the whole time, even when she knows she's in the wrong. She fights and fights, and nine times out of 10 it gets her nowhere, just a lot of aggro and tears and slamming doors. The more I see this, the more I think there has to be another way: why go through all that drama and energy just to find that nothing's changed? So when I come across a problem, something I want to do but I'm not allowed to, I start to think my way around things so I can do what I want without getting caught. Because that's what it's about, right? Not getting caught. If you don't get caught then you can do what you want.

Weekends at Mum's, sleeping in until lunchtime if I want and with no one to tell me what to do, but all the time the clock ticking down to Sunday evening and back to the war zone with Dad and Christine.

'Ah, you're making everything messy,' Mum says, but always with a smile. On Monday morning, after Sandra and I have gone back, she'll go right round the house, top to bottom, until everything's spotless. She'll dust, clean, iron and wash, and it'll make her the happiest woman in the world. She'd do all those things even if no one had stepped inside the place from one week to the next.

*   *   *

I'm six. My dad takes me in the car one day.

'Where are we going?'

'Pony club.'

'What's that?'

I soon find out what it is. It's the worst thing in the world. It's me and lots of girls. I want to be out playing football and climbing trees with my friends.

'You have to stay here.'

'Why?'

'Because I say so.'

This is my life for a while: school, ponies, home, a circuit on endless repeat. Sometimes I hear a word on the TV news or whispered between adults when they think I'm not listening. Rapire. I don't know what it means. Rapire.

Someone eventually explains it to me. It's called kidnapping, they say. Bad people take rich people and only give them back to their families in exchange for lots of money.

But we're not rich, I say.

No. But your dad's well known, so the bad people might think he's rich. That's why he's so protective of you.

* * *

Dad buys me jodhpurs, boots and a riding jacket.

'You have to look the part,' he says.

He takes me to an enormous set of stables full of movement and noise: the whinnying of horses, the shouts of the lads, the clanging of pails. It's huge, frightening, but my dad doesn't seem scared so I know he'll want me not to be scared too.

'This is Signor Cumani,' he says. 'Signor Cumani trains all the horses here.'

'And your father rides the best ones for me!' Sergio Cumani replies. 'Maybe one day you'll be a jockcy like him.'

I don't want to be a jockey. I want to be a petrol pump attendant. Get a uniform, see all those flash cars – and in any case, the price of petrol is very high, so I'll get rich, right?

Signor Cumani moves among the horses after exercise, feeding them sugar lumps and examining them closely. One of the lads lifts me onto the back of one that's tired and being walked round the yard while it cools off. I'm so light that I just cling to the horse's mane, but the lad holds my leg just in case.

I watch Niki Lauda become Formula One world champion in his Ferrari with two races still to go. It's the third year in a row that Ferrari have won the constructors' championship, and every schoolboy in the land has a Ferrari poster on their wall. I tell myself that I'll have a Ferrari by the time I'm 30.

I want to go out and play in the garden, but Christine won't let me. 'Your father's resting. He can't be disturbed.'

Sandra does her best to protect me. If necessary she lies for me, not just because I'm her little brother, but also because she gets punished on her own account so often that a bit more makes no real difference to her: may as well be hung for a sheep as a lamb and all that.

'Lanfranco?'

'Yes?'

We're whispering because it's late and Sandra doesn't want to be overheard.

'Can you keep a secret?'

'Sure.'

'I'm going back to Mum's.'

'This weekend?'

'No. Sooner. To live there. I can't stand it here any more. I'm going to get my stuff together and then I'll be gone before he knows it.'

I lie in the dark and wonder whether she'll go through with it.

*   *   *

She does go through with it. She goes to school and doesn't come home, simple as that.

Dad goes ballistic. The kitchen is practically rocking with the force of the argument, accusations flying every which way: who knew beforehand, whose fault it is, who drove her away, whether to go and get her back, and on and on.

I go to bed alone that night. No big sister, no protector. I'm eight years old, alone in a house with a father who barely talks to me and a stepmother who seems determined to make my life a misery.

The next afternoon – the very next afternoon – Dad's at the school gates at the end of the day, waiting for me in a horsebox. He's never done this before.

I sprint across the road, climb into the front seat and give him a big kiss.

'I'm going to give you a big surprise,' he says.

We set off through the streets of Milan and out into the suburbs.

'Your sister, she's a bad girl, you know,' he says. 'The way she's behaved, that's not how you should behave. You know that?'

I nod.

We keep on driving until we reach a field with three ponies: two bays and a palomino.

My father gestures at them. 'You choose.'

'That one.' I point straight to the palomino, of course, looking almost otherworldly with its white face, mane and tail.

'Lanfranco, meet Silvia, your new pony. You will look after her. After school you will come to muck her out, feed her and ride her. She's your responsibility now.'

We take Silvia home and put her in a field just down the road from our house. And every day after school I'm as good as my word: I muck her out, feed her and ride her. I start to bring all my mates from school to watch me ride her round the field, pretending to be a jockey. The ponies at pony club a couple of years before weren't mine, and there were too many girls there. But Silvia's mine, there are no girls here, and I love her.

This is the moment that horses become my life.

I'm just about nine when I ride a pony derby at the San Siro track in Milan. To me it feels like the greatest race on earth, and I've trained on Silvia in the field at home for weeks on end, but all the other ponies are giants compared to Silvia and all the other jockeys are giants compared to me. We fall behind pretty much from the start, and when Silvia sees the crowd at the finish line she digs in her toes and sends me sprawling into the water jump. I'm dead last and soaked through. It doesn't put me off.

'I want to be a jockey,' I tell my dad.

He takes me to see a back specialist, who X-rays me and measures the cartilage between my bones to give an accurate estimation of my expected growth.

'The boy will grow too tall to be a jockey,' says the doctor.

'I'm going to be a jockey,' I say.

If Dad's impressed by my determination, he doesn't show it.

I'm 10. We drive from Milan to Rome for the Italian Derby and walk the track on the morning of the race. Dad stops to chat to a bunch of English jockeys, one of whom doesn't look much older than me.

'Who was that?' I ask when we've said our goodbyes and are walking on.

'He's called Walter Swinburn.'

'Is he good?'

'He's one of the most natural horsemen you'll ever see.'

He opens a glossy racing magazine and points to a picture of Lester Piggott, stone-faced and inscrutable as a sphinx.

'Look at him,' says Dad. 'You could be just as success-ful if you work hard enough.'

Italian TV shows lots of races from around the country, but only four from abroad: the Grand National, the Epsom Derby, the King George and the Arc. The Grand National is totally crazy, too crazy for me. It's the Derby that gets me. It's like watching something from outer space: the crowds, the horses, the colours. In Milan most races have eight horses at most, and here's this race with what looks like 20 or 30 in it.

'I want to ride in that race one day,' I tell my dad.

Dad's off to this black-tie jockey gala, some big annual dinner. He brings out this white-gold Piaget watch from the 1960s. It's the most beautiful thing I've ever seen. A rich owner gave it to him once for winning a race, and he treasures it like it's the Crown Jewels of the Queen of England. For 364 days a year he keeps it in the safe, and for one night only he brings it out.

He smiles like the cat who got the cream and dangles the watch in front of my face.

'If you win the Epsom Derby,' he says, 'I'll give you this.'

*   *   *

I'm 13: totally addicted to racing, mad keen to become a jockey and finding school increasingly tedious. I can leave school this coming summer for good, if my parents let me.

Dad sits me down.

'You're sure about this?' he says.

'Absolutely.'

'You know this isn't going to be easy?'

'I know.'

'You know or you *know*? Because you need to *know*. It's going to test your resolve to the absolute limit. For every small boy who sets out to become a jockey, only one in a thousand makes it. Why should that be you? Are you motivated enough? Aggressive enough? I wonder, sometimes. You're a quiet boy. Meek, almost.'

In your presence, yes, I think. *That's because I feel intimidated by you. Away from home there are plenty of people to testify that I'm almost too exuberant. At school I'm known as the naughtiest boy in the class.*

I say the only thing I can. 'Why shouldn't it be me?'

I start off in Milan, at Alduino and Giuseppe Botti's yard. I turn up on the first morning in my immaculate jodhpurs and flashy jacket, five stone sopping wet and the stable jockey's son, so they all take one look at me and think what a prize chump I am. I'm not strong enough or experienced enough to ride big, hard-pulling thoroughbreds, and because of who my dad is they're scared of treating me badly, taking any risks with me or making me do the dirty or dangerous jobs normally reserved for newcomers. But these are the things I want, and more to the point these are the things I need: to be pushed, to be challenged, to improve.

Dad turns up every few days to check up on me, and every time he sees me he immediately starts shouting, 'Let your leathers down, you're riding too short, keep your bum down, try to look tidy. Do this, do that, do the other.' I try to take it all in, but most of it goes in one ear and out the other by the time I climb onto another horse and start making the same mistakes all over again. Whatever I do doesn't seem to satisfy him, and the shouting just makes me go into my shell.

The Bottis' yard, like all the ones in Milan, closes down in late autumn, so Dad sends me to work for Tonino Verdicchio at his winter training quarters in Pisa, three hours' drive to the south. It's the furthest I've ever been from home, by a long way, and it feels like he's sending me to the moon. Tonino is one of his oldest friends, and Dad asks just two things of him: work Lanfranco hard and pay him peanuts.

That's just what Tonino does. But he also shows me great warmth, as do his wife Antonietta and their three daughters. The girls give me a hard time, but I know they do so with affection. When I fall off the horses, Tonino just shrugs his shoulders and laughs. He doesn't yell, doesn't judge me, doesn't make me think I'm useless. He doesn't try to overload me with information I can't keep track of. He gives me the one thing I need most of all, and that's confidence. Within six weeks I'm riding on his better horses alongside decent jockeys, and in the three or four months I'm with him I learn more about horses than I have in all my life before that put together.

I learn more about life, too. I've basically been an only child for a long time, for five years or so, since Sandra left to live with Mum. But Tonino and Antonietta, they treat me as their son, and the girls treat me as their brother. I've always been in my shell, but now the shell breaks and a different person comes out – or maybe the real person comes out, the person who's been there all along.

By the time it comes for me to head back to Milan in the spring I'm genuinely bereft.

I'm back at the Bottis' yard, thinking I might be able to make a go of this after all. Be a jockey here in Italy, ride 30, 40 winners a year. Nothing like my old man, but then in lots of ways I am nothing like my old man.

Dad sees the change in me, on and off the horse. He can hardly not.

Dad and Christine sit me down.

'You're going to England to work at Luca's,' Dad says. Luca's a trainer there. It was his father Sergio's stables that Dad took me to when I was little and the lad lifted me up onto the horse.

'What?'

'You heard.'

'That's ... no. I'm riding well, I've got all my friends here. Why am I going to England?'

'Because you're going to be champion jockey, and going there's vital for that. Nowhere like England to learn what you still need to learn.'

They've got it all figured out. Every objection I raise, they've got an answer. No, they won't come with me. Yes, it is all organised. No, I don't get to refuse. Yes, it will be good for me. No, I don't speak any English. Yes, I'll be able to learn some.

It's 10 July 1985, three days before the Live Aid concert, which everyone's already talking about. I get on a plane from Milan to Luton with a tag round my neck like Paddington Bear, because I'm 14 years old and an unaccompanied minor. I've got a bucketful of dreams in my head and a million lira in my pocket, which sounds a lot but equates to just over £350. As the plane claws its way into the sky I feel as if I'm an astronaut heading for the stars. My life is changing for ever, and I have no control over it.

Luca's chauffeur David meets me at the airport. He doesn't speak any Italian and I don't speak any English, but he smiles and does his best to make me welcome. We listen on the car radio to the July race meeting at Newmarket, and I hear the commentators talking about a horse named Lanfranco. Suddenly I don't feel quite so far from home.

I live in a bed and breakfast, in a room under the corner of the roof next to the main road. It's not much bigger than a broom cupboard, with just enough space for a small bed, a sink and a cupboard. The orange squash comes out of a plastic bottle and ravioli comes from a tin. They're both disgusting.

Some of Luca's other lads are living in the same place.

'What's your name?' they ask.

'Lanfranco.'

'Yer what?'

'Lanfranco.'

'We can't pronounce that. Too much of a mouthful. We'll call you Frankie.'

I cry myself to sleep that night, and for quite a few nights after that too.

Luca's yard is way bigger than anything I've ever seen before in racing. He has a hundred horses, half of them in the main yard beside the house and the rest in the bottom yard where I start.

And it's not just this yard that's huge. All of Newmarket is full of horses: being led by their lads across the roads, working up on the heath, being loaded in and out of horseboxes. There are more than 60 sets of stables here. Sometimes it seems like a horse town where humans are allowed in rather than vice versa.

I'm several years younger than any of the other lads, who either ignore or bully me, and since I can't speak the language I can't answer back. In Italian I'm quick-witted and always able to parry a verbal barb with one of my own. Here I might as well be a mute. That's the law of the jungle, the way it is in racing: the youngest and weakest learn the hard way, and as they grow stronger, they in turn make life difficult for the latest newcomers.

I'm keen as mustard. Every morning I'm up so early I arrive at the yard before the head lad, so I'm usually the one who opens up the tack room. The only one who talks to me is a nice old boy called George Dunwoody, who looks after Commanche Run, winner of last year's

St Leger, and who has trained and ridden horses in Northern Ireland for many years. We're like the odd couple, thrown together by fate: the young Italian nuisance at the start of his career and the veteran stableman helping out around the yard at the other end of the line. George always has time for me and tries to explain things as best he can through the language barrier. We sit outside on a couple of bales of straw most mornings, eating breakfast together.

Everyone calls Luca 'guv'nor', and it's clear he expects things to be done properly. All the lads seem in awe of him as he moves around the yard like a Roman emperor or a dictator, very cold and professional. At evening stables he runs his finger along the top of my horse's back and holds it up to show the dirt on its coat I haven't cleaned off.

'I'm too short to reach its back.'

'Then stand on a bucket.'

He checks the next night, too. He's a master of his trade, and I'm not living up to his standards.

My dad rings once a week, on a Monday at exactly 7 p.m. The first time I pick up, I'm in tears before he starts speaking.

'Dad, this is awful, it's a nightmare. You've got to let me come home.'

'You said you'd do whatever it took, son.'

'But not this.'

'You want to have a big car and fly in private planes like Lester Piggott and Pat Eddery? Then this is what it takes.'

Every Monday he phones, and every Monday we have the same conversation.

'Stick at it,' he says. 'It will get better.'

And you know what? It does. I start to learn a bit of English. The guys who bullied me now see that I'm still here and haven't gone under. They become my friends, two of them in particular: Colin Rate and Andy Keates.

'It's weird,' I say. 'My English is getting better and I can understand Andy perfectly well, but with Colin, I still can't make out a single word.'

'Ah,' says Andy. 'There's a reason for that.'

'What's that?'

'He's from Sunderland.'

We go out on Saturday nights into the Newmarket pubs. There are always rivalries with other stables, of course: their lads against ours. If a lad from another stable picks on me – which they do, as I'm so small and look way too young to be served alcohol, despite the newsprint I rub on my top lip to try to make it look like

I've got bumfluff – Luca's lads instantly rally round and circle the wagons to protect me. They might still give me shit every day at work, but I'm one of them now, and you defend your team against the world.

'You know my son Richard's doing well on the jumps,' George says one day.

'Is he?'

'He's going to get another go at the National next year on West Tip.' West Tip fell at Becher's six months ago while in the lead.

'What are the odds?'

'At the moment? 33/1.' I raise my eyebrows. 'It's a steal at that price, Frankie, an absolute steal. Get in there now and surf those odds all the way down as they narrow over the winter.'

I go down to Cuthie Suttle's betting shop on the high street and put £50 on.

We crowd round the TV to watch the Grand National. West Tip is by now second favourite at a starting price of 15/2. I've surfed the odds all the way down through the winter, just as George told me I would. Now all his boy has to do is win.

I've never been so nervous watching a race in my entire life. The whole stables know what I stand to win, and they live every moment with me. West Tip bides his time before moving up in the closing stages, and as he jumps the last, neck and neck with Young Driver, I can hardly watch.

Slowly, slowly, West Tip edges ahead as they race towards the Elbow. 'West Tip by two lengths from Young Driver!' yells Peter O'Sullevan on commentary. 'West Tip by *three* lengths from Young Driver!'

Ecstasy! I go mad, absolutely mental: leaping around the place, high-fiving everyone, hugging, kissing, crying. I can't believe there's a happier man in England right now, including George and Richard.

I collect my winnings from Cuthie Suttle and fold the notes over so they make a big bulge in my pocket: £50 at 33/1 plus my original stake back makes £1,700. I feel like a millionaire. In the snooker clubs I play on the £5 tables and act like I'm Alex Higgins.

I buy a Vespa so I can scoot around Newmarket quicker – it's white, which is to say dark grey after a week in Newmarket weather – and a new washing machine for my landlady Mrs Sykes, as hers is on its last legs, not least from having to wash all my stinky clothes for months on end.

Then I begin the process of giving all the winnings back to Mr Suttle in the time-honoured fashion: by making bad bet after bad bet. Soon I haven't just lost all the money I have, but quite a lot of the money I don't.

I go to Luca. 'Guv'nor, could you give me an advance on my wages so I can pay off my gambling debts?'

'Stable lads get paid every Friday, Frankie.'

'I know that. I'm just asking if –'

'Stable lads get paid every Friday, Frankie.'

When I next speak to my dad I ask if he can wire me some money. I know what his response will be before I even ask.

I go back to Mr Suttle and agree to work as a board chalker in the afternoons, putting up the odds. He won't pay me, but he'll take off what would have been my wages from what I owe until we're square again.

I chat to the punters when they come in and as they're watching the races. One day a chap called Pete Burrell comes in. He's an assistant trainer for Julie Cecil.

'I know you,' he says. 'You're the gobby Italian who always shouts things at us when we pass you in the strings up on the Heath.'

That's me, always desperate to be noticed. I wear flamboyant colours, I'm cheeky, I shout at people, I do my own thing. People love me, they hate me, but they can't ignore me.

'Yeah,' I reply. 'And I'm also the gobby Italian who's going to win his apprentice race tomorrow.'

Pete cocks his head a moment and looks at me.

'You're going to be champion jockey one day,' he says. 'And I'm going to be your manager.'

The police catch me riding my moped on the pavement. Mrs Sykes tells them I don't speak any English and don't know the rules. They let me off.

'Thanks, Mrs Sykes,' I say when they're gone. 'But I do speak some English now, you know.'

'Yes,' she replies. 'Mainly swear words.'

Lester watches me riding one day. It's like having God cast his eye over you.

He thinks I have a big man's hands. Same kind of thing the back specialist said in Italy: I'm going to grow too tall and heavy to be a jockey. But if I don't, he reckons I'll be one of the best ever. Already I've got two years on other riders my age, as I've had those two years working while they've been in school.

I'm 15 years and 6 months old, which means I'm old enough to race in Italy. Dad flies me over to Milan, where he's entered me in a race. There are just eight runners, and four of them are Dettoris: my uncle, my dad, my cousin and me. Dad and I are riding for the same stable and the same owner, so as far as the punters are concerned we're coupled: if you bet on either of us you get your money, even if the other person wins.

So we're racing and I'm leading, no idea how. We come round the turn and into the home straight, and all I can hear is Dad shouting, 'Come on! Push it! Kick it! Push it!' He's behind me, and another jockey – one of the four I'm not related to – is slowly passing me on the right. I get my head down and just keep riding, doing the best I can.

All of a sudden, on the outside, boom! Dad goes and wins. The other guy's second, I finish third. And I'm thinking, *Well, I haven't done too badly.*

We're walking back in after the race, and I realise that everybody's crying with laughter.

Jeez, I think, *did I look that bad? Did I really look that bad?*

I walk into the changing rooms and watch the replay. Now I see why they're all laughing. Halfway into the straight, Dad started whipping *my* horse to make it run faster.

The stewards call us in.

'Well, Mr Dettori,' they say to Dad. 'We know he's your son, but you can't ride a horse for him.'

But that's Dad. He just wants me to win so badly.

* * *

I'm 16. Dad breaks his left leg in two places when his horse crashes into a concrete post in Milan. Three days later I'm riding at Goodwood on a filly called Lizzy Hare, named after Luca's secretary who drives me to the course. Colin leads the horse up, but more eyes are on him than her, as he's wearing a lurid black suit with pink seams, a pink shirt, pink tie and pink socks.

'Hey, Colin?'

'What?'

'John Travolta called. He wants his suit back.'

Lizzy Hare's got no chance here, I think. She's 12/1 and there are three champion jockeys in the race: Steve Cauthen, Willie Carson and Pat Eddery. I tuck in behind Willie on Betty Jane before Steve takes over with a strong run on Interlacing. For a brief moment there are five fillies spread across the course, but Lizzy Hare is finding plenty for me and squeezes through a gap on the far rail to take the prize by a length and a half from Interlacing.

I act as though I've won the Triple Crown. I'm thrilled to win, even more pleased to beat Steve, as he's long been a hero of mine, and I'm made up for Colin, who's backed Lizzy Hare and has landed a nice little touch.

In the car on the way home, I take a box of tissues and a pen.

Frankie Goes to Hollywood, I write.

* * *

At last I'm on my way, but for those expecting a sudden rash of winners, well, it doesn't happen. One swallow does not a summer make and all that. The reality is that I'm an Italian learning my trade in a foreign country, so just to be getting a few rides is good.

I don't panic, quite the opposite. The win on Lizzy Hare and the way I'm riding in general gives me this inner belief that I'm going to make it. There is absolutely no doubt in my mind. My father's been brainwashing me for so long during our weekly phone conversations that I've actually begun to believe him.

I go to America once the season's over, to work for Richard Cross in Santa Anita, and quickly fall in love – not with a girl, or even a horse, but with the way the jockey Angel Cordero rides. He's a real showman, a crowd-pleaser who always gets the spectators out of their seats, and when he wins he doesn't just get off the horse as normal, but does a flying dismount, using his irons as a springboard and jumping high in the air before landing.

In the privacy of Richard's barn I indulge my fantasies by practising my own flying dismounts in front of a baffled audience of a few Mexican horse walkers and grooms. I'm not bad, even if I say so myself. My mum's passed on the suppleness, athleticism, agility and balance I need to be a jockey.

But the drive and ambition? They're all Dad's.

I come back from the pub late one Friday night. There's something called *After Dark* on Channel 4, a discussion programme, and this week they're talking about racing. John McCririck's on it, so too the Duchess of Argyll and a few other people. Most of them are talking a load of rubbish, but there's this one guy called Barney Curley who catches my attention. He doesn't say much, but whenever he speaks it's always worth hearing. He knows more than the rest of them put together.

A month later I'm at Tattersalls for the sales, and Barney's there.

'I want you to ride one for me next week,' he says. 'Don't tell your agent. Just tell him not to book a ride for you in that race.'

It's the start of a beautiful friendship. Barney's a character, and then some. He made millions back in the seventies through landing a massive gamble on his own horse Yellow Sam at Bellewstown. He knew Yellow Sam was much better than the bookies thought, so in an operation of military precision he got a group of his friends to back the horse at 20/1 in betting shops all round Ireland. Naturally the off-course bookies tried desperately to phone their counterparts on the course and tell them to shorten the price, but these were the days before mobile phones. There was only one phone box on the course, and Barney's enormous mate Benny O'Hanlon blocked that for the final 25 minutes before the race. Barney made *millions*. It was one of the great coups of modern times. Later he made another fortune by selling his Georgian mansion near Mullingar in County Westmeath via a nationwide raffle, and saw off the taxman when he inevitably came sniffing round.

I love being around people like Barney, captivated by their personalities, their stories, their experiences.

I'm due to ride an apprentice race at Newmarket. Luca asks Ray Cochrane whether he should get Pat to ride for him at Haydock. Ray nods in my direction. 'Let Frankie ride,' he says.

Ray won the Derby on Kahyasi. He knows his horses and he knows his jockeys. For him to big me up like this means a lot and is a real vote of confidence.

The life of a jockey is measured out by the same routes to the same racecourses, time after time. I can already give you directions to most of the courses in England with my eyes shut.

I'm at Catterick riding Torkabar, one of the Aga Khan's horses. He's the red-hot favourite to win an uncompetitive maiden, but he's also a monkey who threw away victory in our previous race at York by veering violently in the closing stages. Once again he's determined not to put his best foot forward, and the more I ask, the more he resists. This is one of the real tests a jockey can face: anyone can ride a horse which races smoothly and easily, but dealing with one who just doesn't want to be there and won't play ball really sorts the men from the boys. Today I'm not up to the task. Just after we pass the line a well-beaten third, I lash out with my whip in temper and strike Torkabar over the head. It's pure frustration – I've lost my rag – and it's also totally wrong. You don't hit horses on the head – you just don't.

I'm hauled up before the stewards, and instead of coming clean and accepting my weakness, I try to save face. 'I gave him a tap to prevent him ducking through a gate towards the paddock,' I say.

It's horseshit, and they know it as well as I do. They ban me for three days for improper riding.

The next morning I'm in the doorway of a stable in Luca's bottom yard, half-heartedly scratching around in the straw with a pitchfork. Suddenly Ray's leaning over me, going absolutely mad, shouting and screaming that I've let the side down.

'Hitting any horse over the head is bang out of order. But to do it to one belonging to the Aga Khan – are you out of your fucking mind? He's the principal owner of this place. He's just about the biggest name in racing. Without him, we wouldn't have jobs. So stop being such a fucking idiot.'

Luca's away in America at the sales, but when he returns, he also lets me have it with both barrels and promptly suspends me from riding for two weeks. A fortnight on the sidelines at this stage, when I'm progressing every day, seems like a lifetime. That's the point.

I end up riding 22 winners from 140 mounts in 1988, a decent rate of return by any standards other than the very highest.

There's a message for me: *Ring your father. Urgently.*

'Dad? What's up?'

'I've been speaking to Luca over the past couple of days.'

'And?'

'And he wants you to be stable jockey next year.'

Stable jockey. The one who gets the pick of a stable's rides, and as much to the point gets guaranteed rides too. In a world where most jockeys have to hustle for rides each and every day, being a stable jockey is the nearest thing you get to a salaried job, not to mention the kudos it gives: that a trainer who knows his onions reckons you've got what it takes.

'Lanfranco? Did you hear me?'

'Yes, I heard. I'm just … a bit shocked, that's all.'

I let him talk, not just for what he says, but also so I can revel in the pride in his voice. It's not often that I hear it, and when I do it's like the sun is shining down just on me. But what he says is important too. 'The fact that you're only 18 and still so inexperienced is bound to count against you with some of the more prominent owners in the yard. That's just the way it is. Don't take it personally. Just show them what you can do. And remember that you're going to be in the spotlight like never before. Every move, every mistake, people will be watching. The time for fooling around is over, Lanfranco.'

Gerald Leigh, who breeds many of the horses which find their way to Luca's stable, says something similar. 'It's a great job, Frankie, even though it might have come a year too soon. So be careful. It's like picking up a knife. If you pick it up by the handle then you're fine, but pick it up by the blade and it can scar you for life.'

*   *   *

I trade in my crappy old Mazda 323 for a Mercedes 190 with all the extras: body kit, wheels, spoilers and a stereo that could wake the dead. Gangsta rap and bling are all the rage right now, but even some rappers would hesitate before speccing their cars like this.

I think it looks fabulous. Everyone else thinks that the only thing which looks more ridiculous than the car is me when I sit in it.

I want to be famous. I want to be with the A-list. If I ride well enough then I'll get recognised, and if I'm recognised, I can use that to propel me into that world. I'm a show-off. I love it when the world looks at me. I live in Newmarket where nothing goes on. I want to be in London where it's all happening. I want more. There's a whole world out there that I want to see, the world in tabloids and magazines which looks so glorious and glamorous and luxurious.

The Met Bar. Everyone talks about the Met Bar, everyone goes to the Met Bar, everyone is *seen* at the Met Bar. So that's where I go. And people do recognise me, because racing's huge: all the taxi drivers, all the people who work in restaurants, they spend half the day in the bookies. So when I come to London and people recognise me, I grow a foot taller. I feel great, I can go anywhere – it's like someone's handed me the keys to the city.

This kid who wasn't allowed out for fear of being kidnapped as a boy, who grew up as more or less an only child, who knows stables and racecourses and horseboxes but not much else … this kid wants more.

What that 'more' actually means, though, what I'm really looking for, I don't know.

Lester makes a comeback at 55 after five years away from the track and a year inside. I'm in his face all the time, telling him he should be in a museum, advising him to get the slippers out because there's no way he'll be able to keep up with us young bucks.

We're riding at Glorious Goodwood. There's a big field, 20 runners or so. As we come into the bend at the halfway point, furthest from the stands, I glance to my left and see him half a length behind me. He reaches over, grabs my balls and squeezes as hard as he can. The pain's extraordinary: I feel my eyes watering behind my goggles.

'That'll teach you to be cocky, you little shit,' he says.

After the race, back in the weighing room, we watch a replay. I gather everyone round. 'Lads,' I say, 'watch out for where Lester grabs my balls. It's coming up round about now.'

There's a blind spot in the coverage of about 10 seconds, where the cameras switch and the action's too far away to be caught by either of them. It's in those 10 seconds that the cunning old fox made his move on my meat and two veg. He knows exactly where the cameras are, of course. He knows everything.

I look across at him. Not a trace of a smirk passes his lips.

I take a heavy fall on a horse called Muirfield Village at Sandown. He clips the heels of the horse in front, stumbles and sends me flying. We both escape without lasting harm, but Luca lays into me. 'I don't care if you hurt yourself. I can find other jockeys in a heartbeat. But I do care if you hurt a horse, no matter who he belongs to. And if you keep riding like that, too close behind the ones in front and cutting through their hind legs, you will maim one of them sooner or later. You're too cocky, too stupid, not experienced enough. You're always going a stride too far, getting in too tight, poking into places where you shouldn't go. You know how far a horse's legs can extend at full gallop. Respect that.'

* * *

I end up with 75 wins in 1989 and the title of champion apprentice. Not bad for my first season as stable jockey. I set my cap for next season at 100 winners. It's ambitious – no teenager's done it since Lester 35 years ago – but in the end I make it with months to spare. The ton comes up on 27 August, at Chepstow on Line of Thunder. Lester had taken two months longer.

Not long after, I win on Henryk at Nottingham for Barney Curley. Henryk hasn't won for ages and is hardly in the first flush of youth, but heck, nothing ventured, nothing gained. My instructions are to drop him out towards the rear, then wait until the last moment before popping him in front on the line. I carry out my orders to the letter, coming fast and late to snatch the lead in the final strides.

'I thought Frankie had left it too late,' Barney tells the press. 'He nearly gave me a heart attack. But he knew what he was doing. He'll be champion jockey one day, mark my words.'

Winners are all very well, but there are hierarchies in racing, just as there are anywhere else. At the top of the tree are the five Classics – the 1000 Guineas, 2000 Guineas, Derby, Oaks and St Leger. Then there are the Group 1 races for the best horses, followed by Group 2 and Group 3. Just under 40 races a year are counted as

Group 1, and though I've been trying for two seasons, I've yet to win any of them.

My love affair with Ascot is already underway. It's the Ascot festival towards the end of September, and I win three on the Thursday and another on the Friday. Now, on the Saturday, I'm riding Markofdistinction in the Queen Elizabeth II Stakes, one of the richest races of the season. He's only fifth favourite, but he's got a searing turn of pace and I reckon that could be decisive – if I dare wait long enough to deliver it.

I drop him out last of all in the early stages as Steve Cauthen takes us along smartly on Shavian. I start to close up, ready to strike, but that canny bugger Pat Eddery's there already, edging right-handed across me and stealing first run on my outside. I've got five strides, six at the most, before the door's shut for good, and if that happens then our impetus will go and so will the race. At times like this you discover the difference between a very good horse and a champion.

'Go on, boy,' I say. 'Show me what you've got.'

Markofdistinction takes off as if scalded, squeezing through the gap a moment before it disappears. Distant Relative still holds a slender lead with a furlong to run, but I know the race is already over: nothing can match Markofdistinction's blinding pace over a furlong, and he bounds ahead to claim a famous victory by a length.

The moment I cross the line will live with me for ever. Suddenly, for a few startling seconds, the world turns dark. All I can see is a mass of flames around me, as if the place is on fire. I'm the only one moving at normal speed: everything else is in slow motion, almost stopping. Then someone turns the lights on again and I'm back in the world, overwhelmed at what I've just achieved.

By the time the season's ended, I've won 141 races, almost exactly double last year's total.

Out in America, Angel Cordero invites me to dinner after the Breeders' Cup. Just for once I try to listen instead of doing all the talking.

'You've got to ride with just your toes in the stirrups,' he says.

'That's not how we Europeans ride.'

'I know. You shove your feet in as far as they'll go, so the iron's beneath the midpoint of your foot, the arch. But when you go on tiptoes, when you dance, when you play tennis, where do you push off from?'

'The ball of the foot.'

'Exactly. That's where all the feeling and balance are.'

He takes me to his gym to give a practical demonstration on his own mechanical horse. He shows me what to do, looking smooth and sleek and so stylish. Then he jumps off and invites me to have a go.

I look and feel really awkward in comparison. 'It's so strange,' I say. 'And it's killing my calf muscles.'

'Of course it is. You've been riding all your life one way. It's bound to hurt when you start doing it a different way. You're using muscles you don't normally use. Stick with it and it'll get better, I promise.'

Instead of going back to America after the 1991 season, I go to Hong Kong. It's maximum city, full on all day, every day. I love its buzz, the pandemonium at the tracks and the frantic pace of the night life. I also take the chance to experiment by riding with my toes in the irons, the way Angel showed me. I'd be much too shy to try it at home, but I assume nobody will be watching me ride my work horses out here too closely.

At first it's absolute agony, proper killing me, with the pain sharpest in my calves. Every day I'm tempted to give it all up and go back to the method I know and trust, but every day I make myself persevere through the worst of the pain. Eventually I work up to 10 horses a day with my toes in the irons, and soon I've got thicker muscles in my calves and an extra, unexpected lump of muscle on top of my feet.

I also discover that my new riding position leads to a different rhythm through a race. When you ride with your feet fully in the irons your sense of balance is very much on the horse's mouth. With just your toes in the stirrup irons and the saddle well forward, the horses jump from the gate and go, so you're not pulling on the horse's mouth nearly so much. But if you sit too low on a horse too early in a race, all that horse will want to do is take off with you. I start combining the best of both worlds: ride a bit higher in the first half of a race to keep the horse relaxed, and then switch to a lower, tighter crouch in the second half.

It's 1992, the fourth season I've been Luca's stable jockey, and the wheels are coming off. Part of it is that we're seriously short of decent horses and winners, but part of it is my doing too. I've got bundles of money and a name for myself, I'm 21 and I want to be out on the town all night, every night rather than sitting at home with a glass of carrot juice and a lettuce leaf. Life is not a dress rehearsal, that's my motto: I want to play as hard as I work. But I haven't got the balance right between self-denial and letting off steam, and something has to give.

At a deeper level, I feel that I'm outgrowing our partnership, or perhaps more precisely that the partnership as it is no longer reflects the reality of our roles. I've worked for Luca for seven years. Once I was the naughty new kid, the one who was always getting into trouble.

Now I'm one of the best jockeys in the country, but somehow we've both failed to adjust to my new status. I'm not even sure exactly what I'm searching for, but I do know beyond doubt that I have to try my luck elsewhere. Unless I raise my sights, I'll never cross the gulf which still separates me from the greatest riders in the world.

Most other jockeys would probably settle for what I'm preparing to throw away. Even when things aren't going so well for him, Luca's still one of the country's best trainers – astute, hard-working and ambitious. But settling isn't in my nature. Seven years ago my dad sent me to Luca because he wanted more for me than just to be a good jockey in Italy. Now I have to leave Luca because I want more for me than just to be a good jockey in Britain. There's always another mountain to climb.

I ride my first Derby, on Pollen Count for John Gosden. We're 14/1 so I don't expect much, and I don't get much, either: we're 16th out of 20, way off the pace. But that's almost irrelevant in my excitement at being here, riding in the race I used to watch goggle-eyed, back in Milan. I thought the riders looked like they came from Mars: well, that must make me a Martian, because now I'm one of them. The crowds, the attention, the pressure, the excitement, the madness of it all: they're all way, way greater than anything I've ever experienced. No race I've ridden even comes close to this.

I remember my dad waving the Piaget watch in my face.

'If you win the Epsom Derby, I'll give you this.'

Oh, I will, I think. *And so will you. I'll win and you'll give me the watch.*

I spend a couple of months in Hong Kong after the season's done, and I love it so much that I extend my time there well into the New Year. Whatever I do on the track is nothing compared to what I get up to off it. I'm out till dawn every night partying: champagne, girls, all expenses paid, loving every second of it.

I could get used to this, I think. *Stay here, make a fortune. Beautiful place, party city, great weather. No more slogs up the A1 to Catterick on a shitty day.*

The trainer Gary Ng wines and dines me. 'You're a man in demand,' he says. 'I've got a lot of big owners who love the way you ride, love the way you are. They want you riding for them from the start of next season. Here, have a gold watch, just so you know they're serious.'

'How much money are we talking?' I ask.

'Over two years? About a quarter of a million pounds.'

My eyes do that slot-machine thing. Ker-ching! Quarter of a million over two years? I'd be set for life, and even if the riding's not so great, I can always come back to England and pick up where I left off.

I talk to my dad and tell him what they're offering.

'You have to talk to Luca,' he says.

'Yeah, I will. Just let me get it sorted, all signed and sealed.'

But racing's a small world, and everyone talks to everyone. Soon Luca's heard the rumours and is trying to get hold of me. I don't return his calls. I tell myself it's because I want to make sure all the 't's are crossed and the 'i's dotted, but deep down I know it's because I'm scared of what he'll say.

The rumours reach the press, and still Gary and I haven't signed anything. The Hong Kong Jockey Club are still considering my application to ride there full-time, apparently.

The season's about to start back in England. I have to go back and face the music.

* * *

This isn't a conversation I want to have, but it's one I know I must have. I take a deep breath and walk into Luca's office.

'I can't ride for you as stable jockey after this season,' I say. 'I'm going to Hong Kong later in the year, and nothing you can say is going to change my mind.'

Luca goes ballistic. I knew he wasn't exactly going to be thrilled, but the ferocity of his anger takes me aback. He points out my shortcomings, tells me exactly what he thinks of me, and keeps repeating that I'm throwing my life away.

'Hong Kong's for jockeys at the other end of the rainbow,' he says. 'You're much too young to be going there full-time. You're going to mess up everything you've worked for.'

'My mind's made up, Luca.'

He tries to make me reconsider again, and again I tell him my mind's made up.

'I'll ride for you for the next few months, until I go to Hong Kong.'

He suddenly realises he's wasting his breath.

'You must be joking. You'll do no such thing. Go on, get out! I never want to see you again.'

2

RESPONSIBILITY

The split with Luca doesn't make things better: it makes them worse. I ride for other trainers, but my early season drought extends well into May. Rides are scarce, winners as rare as snow in the Sahara. Good friends like Ray and Bruce Raymond can see that I'm miserable and do their best to pump me up. But a patient needs to take his medicine to help him turn the corner, and I'm not helping myself. Where I used to wear a suit to the races, now I'm turning up at the last minute in trainers and tracksuit, showing all the signs of not giving a damn. I'm out clubbing at night, mixing with people I think are my friends. But friends care if I'm late and unprepared for work the next day, and these people couldn't care less. I'm on a dangerous downward spiral: confused, unhappy and uncertain where it leads.

It's not my job I've lost. It's my direction.

* * *

Ever since I became an Arsenal fan I've dreamed of supporting them at Wembley in a cup final. My chance arrives the day after I win four at Newbury, much needed for my confidence. Arsenal are playing Sheffield Wednesday in the final of the Coca-Cola Cup. A party of us from Newmarket have managed to get some tickets, and we set off in a minibus piled high with cases of beer. Colin and I have painted our faces red and white, Arsenal colours.

By the time we get to Wembley I've already worked my way through several cans and some speed I scored off a kid in the toilets at a service station. Then it's onto the nearest pub for a few more drinks, so I'm absolutely on fire by the time the players run onto the pitch. Watching a cup final is one of the great treats of sport, especially when your team wins: and that's just what Arsenal do, smashing Wednesday 2–1. I'm so wired that when I jump in the air for the first goal I land four rows further forward.

We set off back towards Newmarket in high spirits, but then two of the lads decide they want to celebrate in style in London, and I don't need much persuading to join them. We jump out at a set of traffic lights, get the tube into central London and set about painting the town red and white.

Several hours later, totally out of it in a disco near

Oxford Street, I'm in the mood for anything. A guy in the toilets sells me some coke, and for some reason I think it's a great idea to do it not in the toilet like everyone else, but outside in an alley. Yeah, where all the CCTV cameras are. I'm a genius.

We're fooling around in an alleyway outside the club in Falconberg Mews when a torch is flashed in my face. I squint to see who's behind the light. It's a policeman.

No, it's *two* policemen.

'You boys having a good time?' one of them asks.

'Yes.'

'You been drinking?'

'Yes.'

'Anything else?'

'Just drinking.'

'Turn out your pockets.'

I'm fucked.

We turn out our pockets. My pals are clean. I'm not. I've got that wrap of coke, and I can't hide it.

'You're coming with us,' the cops say.

They load me into a van and take me to the nearest police station, Marylebone. A few minutes ago I was drunk as a lord. Now I feel stone cold sober. If this gets out, I could be finished. Yesterday I rode a winner for the Queen. Now I might be about to become a guest at one of her prisons.

I plead with the police to let me off. I'm wasting my breath.

At the station they search me again, take my finger-prints and ask my name.

'Frankie Dettori.'

They look at each other. 'The jockey?' I want to ask how many other pint-sized blokes called Frankie Dettori there can possibly be, but I figure now's not exactly the time. 'Where did you get the drugs?'

'Some guy. I can't remember.'

They leave me in an interview room to stew, and stew I do. I'm scared for my career, my reputation, my future prospects, but all those worries pale into nothing compared to what scares me the most: telling my dad.

Eventually, the cops bail me, kick me out and tell me to come back in three weeks. I wander the streets till I find a taxi that will take me back to Newmarket. I don't even know how much it costs, and I don't care. All I want is to get home, and I cry all the way back. Maybe when I wake up tomorrow morning I'll find it was all just a dream.

For those three weeks till I have to go back to the police station, I live in mortal fear that it will come out. Every day I buy the paper, every day I watch the news. Every day, nothing. Great. Another 24 hours' breathing space.

The fear gnaws at me, gets its tentacles into every part of my life. I pick up a seven-day ban for careless riding at Leicester, then more or less the moment that's done I get another four days for improper use of the whip on Dayflower in the 1000 Guineas. Everything I touch turns to shit. The world's against me. What else can go wrong?

I tell my dad. He goes ballistic. Lanfranco, you're an addict, you need to get help, you're no better than a street junkie, that kind of thing. No, I say, I'm not an addict. I was partying, I was having fun, I was stupid. I don't need help. Not that kind of help, anyway. Not professional medical help, some kind of Priory clinic thing.

In a strange way it's almost a relief to have told him. Sometimes waiting for the worst to happen is worse than it actually happening. If it had never come out then I'd always at some level have been waiting for it to do so, and that's its own kind of stress.

He flies over and tells me he'll stay till the hearing. He also tells me to hire a solicitor pronto, someone who knows the rules and can plead my case.

The lawyer and I go the police station on the appointed day, just us … and three tiers of paparazzi!

I look round, thinking I must be being done at the same time as someone famous, but gradually it dawns on me: no, these guys are all here for me. I want the ground to open and swallow me up. For three weeks I've lived in fear of this coming out. I thought I'd got away with it, at least in terms of public fallout. And now I know in the most emphatic way possible that I haven't.

My lawyer's plan of action is to try to limit the damage to a police caution for being in possession of a controlled drug. That way I won't have to go through the anguish of a further court appearance at a later date.

'It's a long shot,' he says, 'so let me do the talking.'

For once, I'm happy to agree. My mouth is so dry that I don't know that I could speak even if I wanted to.

We gather in a room where a senior police officer reads me the riot act. He explains that if I'm charged with an offence which reaches court, it will seriously affect my chances of getting a visa for working abroad. I sit there, shaking throughout, like a naughty boy up before the headmaster, knowing that my future as a jockey is being decided. My lawyer points out that it's a first offence, the amount found on me was tiny, and that he has plenty of references as to my good character. The police insist that Class A drugs are serious offences which cannot be waved away. It goes back and forth.

Eventually I hear my lawyer say something.

'Yes,' he's saying, 'we'll accept a caution. Thank you.'

I want to cry with relief. I only just stop short of hugging my lawyer. They let me out of the back entrance so I don't have to run the press gauntlet again.

All the way back to Newmarket I feel as though a weight's been lifted. A police caution's serious enough, but compared to some of the scenarios I've played out in my head these past few weeks it's a slap on the wrist.

But I now know for sure that my dream of riding in Hong Kong is over, though it's another fortnight before my worst fears are confirmed in a press statement. The Hong Kong Jockey Club declare that it's not in their interests or mine to have me riding there that season. I think the die was cast even before I was arrested – there are politics in Hong Kong racing, just as there are in every other racing establishment, and I don't know who's been manoeuvring behind the scenes – but a drugs bust is the last straw. Asian countries are really strict on drugs, so they're certainly not going to give me a contract now.

There are two ways I can look at what's happened, I realise. I can just write it off as something unlucky and keep on going, just as I was, or I can treat it as what it is, a wake-up call, and use it to help me change my life for the better. The last thing on my mind has been racing. All I've thought about is partying and chasing the girls. That's why I've ended up lost, on my own. I must have been crazy to let myself slip so far. It's all a mess, but it's a mess for a good reason. What does a man do when he's down? You go to roll up your sleeves, get your arse back to work, get stuck in again.

But this is easier said than done, and turning it around isn't easy. Even a short, sharp shock like this can't totally dent my cockiness, and I wonder whether there's not a happy medium to be found, some balancing act which will allow me to ride well and party hard.

I'm flying back from Goodwood with a party which includes Barney Curley, on whose horse Mt Templeman I've just lost. After we've landed and are just about to get in our cars, he turns to me.

'Are you serious about being a jockey?' he says. 'Or are you just playing at it?'

'I'm very serious.'

'Come round and see me tonight, then, and we'll have a chat over a game of snooker.'

It's not so much an invitation as an order.

I go round that night. He's got a lovely house, an Arts and Crafts place from the turn of the century, originally built for the Earl of Ellesmere and now boasting a swimming pool, stables and an enormous sitting-room-cum-dining-room with half-moon French windows. He talks and I listen, because even someone as dumb and full of myself as I am does sometimes know when to shut up.

'You rode like a prat on Mt Templeman today,' he says, 'and that cost me money. But that's not why I asked you round. The money's neither here nor there. I've been watching you for a long time, Frankie, and you're riding worse and worse at the moment. You're not concentrating. Your heart's not in it. You're going through the motions. All this Jack the Lad stuff, not thinking straight and drifting aimlessly: you're on the brink of ruining your career. This game chews people up and spits them out if they're not careful, and don't think it won't happen to you, because it will if you let it. You're good enough to get away with it for now, but don't think that'll always be the case. You have a great talent, one of the greatest I've ever seen, but you're throwing it all away. You have a God-given ability to ride horses. Do you know what good fortune that is? And the only thing to do with that talent is to express it, nurture it, maximise it. Train properly, eat properly, get enough sleep. Study the form, and properly, not just a once-over with a hangover and a cup of coffee. Don't think how good you are. Think how good you could be.'

We come to a deal. If I show I'm serious about being as good as I can be – and it'll take more than a few fine words over his snooker table: it'll take me showing him over and again rather than just telling him – then he'll do everything he can to help me.

As he walks me out to my car at the end of the evening, he gestures towards the vast expanse of the property.

'What do you think of my place?' he asks.

'I love it. You know I do.'

'You become champion jockey and I'll sell it to you.'

'We're going to come and live with you, Lanfranco,' my Dad says. 'Christine and me, we're coming over. No one's looking after you, and you need someone to look after you.'

He doesn't say the rest because he doesn't have to. You need someone to save you from yourself, or at least from the parts of you which don't know when to stop.

I realise two things. First, that I'm a jockey first and foremost, and this is where I'm happiest: on a horse, in the stables, around other horse people. Second, all those good times I was having: how good were they, really?

Those clubs I was so desperate to get into, where was their soul? Those guys who go there every day and go out every weekend: do they have a job? What's their job, really? What's their contribution to society? If that's it, then whatever I've been chasing just isn't there. It was always my dream to be there, because most people never even get the chance to see it. But there's not much behind the curtain.

I'm riding Azola for David Loder at Haydock, and I'm grumpy as all hell because I'm down to my absolute minimum of 8 stone, 4 pounds. The horse is being led out by a girl who can't be more than 18 or 19. I've seen her once in the stable yard while riding out for David in the morning, but when I asked about her that day the other lads told me in no uncertain terms that she was way too good for me and to stay away from her. She's beautiful, but there's much more to her than that too: a keen intelligence, a deep warmth.

'Allo, darling,' I say. 'Where have you been hiding? What's your name?'

'Catherine,' she says. 'Catherine Allen.'

'Well, Catherine Allen, would you please give me your phone number?'

'You won't remember it.'

'I will.'

She gives it to me.

Azola finishes third. Catherine comes out onto the course to lead her back.

'I can still remember your number,' I say.

'Bet you can't.'

'Bet you I can.' I rattle it off, word perfect.

By the time we reach the enclosure reserved for the placed horses we have a date: or rather, we have an agreement to go on a date, but actually finding a time when I'm around is more tricky.

We end up going to the cinema in Cambridge a few weeks later to see *Made in America*, starring Whoopi Goldberg and Ted Danson. The movie's OK, nothing special, but I don't care. We have fun, chat easily, and I really like her. She's a classics student at Surrey University, but she does a lot of stuff with horses around here, as her dad is one of the premier equine research scientists in the world.

My rift with Luca remains as deep as ever. I feel uneasy whenever I see him at the races, but I can't bring myself to make the first move to heal the wounds between us, and he's certainly not looking to seek me out.

'You should apologise to him, you know,' Barney says. 'You let him down.'

And so it is that one evening at the end of August I find myself sheltering from the rain outside Luca's front door.

He opens it. I give him a sheepish grin. 'Can I come in?'

'Wait there.'

He closes the door in my face.

I wait. And I wait. A year ago, certainly two, I'd have given him 30 seconds and then stormed off in a huff. But I remember what Barney said about letting him down, and I remember my pledge to be as good as I can be, and I figure that this probably comes under both these categories. If Luca wants to make his point by making me wait and making me wet, then I'll accept that.

After a few minutes he opens the door again and offers his hand. 'Come on in.'

The moment we're in his office I say sorry, apologising for the shabby way I left him. 'I was younger and dumber and rash,' I say. 'I felt invincible, but I was also scared of what you'd say. Now, after some hard knocks, I know better.'

It's not a long chat, but as a first step it's enough. As we talk, I feel a flood of relief that I'm being accepted again by the man who's done so much to put me on the map.

'I hope you'll ride for me again,' Luca says.

'I'd like that.'

'But not for another year. Until then, you're on probation.'

Fair enough.

I'm not the easiest boyfriend to have, that's for sure. Sometimes Catherine and I arrange to meet up for a meal, but I ring at the last minute to call it off because I'm too tired or have to waste hard for a ride the next day. Other times I drop her off at her parents' house early in the evening then head home to bed because I have to be up so early in the morning. My racing schedule makes it difficult to plan things on a regular basis, and when I'm tired, I tend to be a bit short with Catherine. All that would put a lot of girls off, but she seems to take it all in her stride. She's not a pushover, not in the slightest: she just appreciates that jockeys aren't, can't be, normal boyfriends in the way other men can.

Barney's been as good as his word in helping me. He's spoken to John Gosden, who trains a lot of horses belonging to Sheikh Mohammed of Dubai. John's looking to retain a jockey solely to ride the Sheikh's horses, and he and Barney reckon I'm the man for the job. It's a risk for John – if I'm not up to it, it'll backfire on him – but he's seen enough to think the chance worth taking.

It takes me about a nanosecond to accept. I've ridden enough for Sheikh Mohammed in the past to know that he's a dynamic figure intent on winning races at the highest level. His outfit Godolphin aren't just here to win the game, they're here to change it. Until the early eighties, racing was run mainly by the aristocracy and the rich, but ever since then the Middle Eastern influence has been gradually increasing.

There are some people in British racing who don't like this, who think that it's just about money, but it's not. Horses are every bit as much a part of Arab culture as they are European, maybe more so in some respects: in fact, the Godolphin stables are named after the Godolphin stallion from the eighteenth century, one of the original three stallions from which all thoroughbreds are descended.

Godolphin's plan is to train all their horses in Dubai over the winter and only bring them back to the UK in the spring. People scoff and say, 'Oh, it'll never work, we've trained horses in winter here for hundreds of years and it works fine.' But horses are trained in warm climates all over the world – California, Australia, Hong Kong and so on – so this line of argument doesn't really stand up. I think it's a mix of three things: people here are set in their ways; they have a sense of superiority and think English racing is unquestionably the best in the world; and they're a little scared that someone might come along and show that different is better after all.

With John's support, this is a job that could lead to the Classics winners I've craved for so long. Six months earlier, I was heading out of control towards the buffers. Now I've managed to scramble aboard an express train going in the right direction.

'What do you want from next season?' John asks.

'To be champion jockey.' Champion jockey is the guy who wins the most races over the course of the season. It's as simple as that. There's no weighting to give Classics more points than other Group 1s, Group 1s more than Group 2s, or Group 2s more than Group 3s. A win is a win is a win. There's no trophy for champion jockey, but it matters very much to everyone in the weighing room. We're a tough and competitive pack, and everyone wants to be top dog. The title comes with swagger and bragging rights, and those are not nothing, not at all.

'What are you prepared to do to get there?'

'Anything legal.'

For a few years now the season has been deemed to start on 1 March at Doncaster, but this coming year every race will count from New Year's Day onwards, which means two months more of meetings on the three all-weather tracks at Lingfield, Southwell and Wolverhampton. If I ride all those I can probably get 50 or so winners on the board before some of the others come back from their holidays, because not everyone will fancy going at it hammer and tongs right from the word go. The Sheikh's horses won't be running in those events, so I get my agent Mattie Cowing to ring all his contacts and get me plenty of decent horses on standby.

But if I'm going to hit the ground running on New Year's Day, if I'm going to show everyone that I'm different, hungrier and much more disciplined than before, then I have to prepare myself in advance: not just physically, but mentally too.

Dad and Christine have a beach house in Agadir on the Moroccan coast. I spend 10 days there, Christmas included, and I'm utterly single-minded. I tell Catherine that we can't spend Christmas together, and if she doesn't like it then tough. It's not that I don't like her – in the three months we've been going out I've been happier than I can ever remember being with a girl – and it's not that I'm trying to test her loyalty. It's just that this is so important to me that I can see no other way than to give myself 100 per cent to it. I have absolute tunnel vision. I'm a racehorse with blinkers on, and nothing is going to interfere with my programme. I know it will be pretty much impossible to lose weight in the cold weather once I return to England, so all my dieting and fitness work have to be completed in the warmer climate of Morocco.

I lock myself away like a monk, and every day is the same. I wake around 10, have one espresso with a sweetener and a large bottle of water, then doze or lounge around in the sun until two in the afternoon. Then I clamp a Walkman to my ears and set off on a long, lonely trek along the beach towards Agadir. Five miles there, five miles back: walking, running, walking, running. It takes me a couple of hours. The last hour late in the afternoon, when the hunger pangs are really kicking in, is always the hardest. I'm starving, absolutely starving, feeling almost like I'm dying from malnutrition. Then I have a bath to revive me while my father cooks my one meal of the day: grilled fish, nearly always sea bass, a good two-pounder, on its own, no oil, salad or potatoes. I chat with Dad and Christine while we eat, and then I get on the scramble bike I've rented, ride into town and phone Catherine from a phone box there.

Wake, walk, eat, sleep. Wake, walk, eat, sleep. Rinse and repeat.

Control your weight, control your life. I'm on the scales first thing every morning.

I can feel myself changing day by day. My face is leaner, the skin drawn tight across my cheekbones like knives. I get on the scales every day, and each time I'm a pound lighter till I'm down to 8 stone, 1 pound, the lightest I've been since my apprentice days. I look at myself in the mirror and examine the man staring back at me, looking for the hardness in his eyes and the set of his jaw.

What are you prepared to do?

Whatever it takes.

I go to the barber's and ask him to give me a grade 2 cut, not quite skinhead but not far off. It completes the look I'm going for, inside and out: a boxer, a soldier, someone to be feared.

I fly back to England on New Year's Eve and go round to John's house. When he opens the door, he doesn't recognise me for a moment: in fact, he tells me later, his first thought is, *The little bastard has sent his cousin to make his excuses.*

'Welcome back,' he says. 'You ready?'

I nod. 'Let's go to war.'

* * *

First day of the year, first meeting of the day, first race of the meeting: the 12.50 at Lingfield. I win on Tiddy Oggie. It's a tiny race – seven horses, £2,600 prize pot – but that's not the point. One race ridden, one race won. Marker set down. This is my year. And for the first two months, this triangle – Lingfield, Southwell, Wolverhampton – is my existence. Often on Saturdays I manage a double shift: Lingfield in the afternoon, evening under the floodlights at Wolverhampton. Sometimes 12 races in all, sprinting out of Lingfield the moment the last race has finished, driving like a maniac round the M25 and up the M40, and making it with a couple of minutes to spare.

Winter weather's much harder to ride in than summer. We go out to the paddock at the last possible minute, freezing to death in our silks and riding breeches, ride, then rush back into the warmth of the weighing room as quickly as we can. Ear muffs, gloves, thermal socks, tights: you name it, I wear it. Many jockeys also wear face masks to protect them from having the sand from the all-weather surface kicked in their faces. I try one too, but find it so difficult to breathe that unless the temperature's really savage, I'd rather have the sand stinging my face. Besides, the stinging reminds me of what I've vowed to do: whatever it takes, whatever discomfort, whatever pain.

I have to tread a fine line between aggression and moderation. If I'm too passive then I'll lose races I should otherwise win, but if I'm too aggressive I'll pick up bans which will also mean missing out on potential wins. In the past, when I've found myself boxed in on the rails, I've been prepared to nudge my way out, maybe catching the attention of the stewards. Now I'm prepared to sit and suffer, even if it costs me a winning chance: better to live to fight another day than spend a week watching in frustration from the sidelines.

I learn the differences between the courses and how best to ride them. Lingfield has especially bad kickback from the surface, with dust and grit flying everywhere, so I have to get out fast each and every time to make sure I'm in the front three and my mount has as clear a run as possible. Wolverhampton's new track has a distinct bias which favours jockeys prepared to go really wide in search of better ground, while Southwell's deep surface is so physically demanding that you can feel like you're treading treacle five furlongs from home. Horses have to be exceptionally fit to win at Southwell. So do their jockeys.

If the boys who regularly earn their bread and butter on the all-weather circuit resent my presence, they don't show it. They know I've been dumped on my arse and am trying to re-establish myself, so I'm just like the rest of them: chasing the winners, riding through the worst of the bad weather to give myself an edge when the turf season begins at Doncaster on 24 March. And when that day comes around, I've got 51 winners already and am leading the pack.

Every morning I have breakfast with John. Well, he has breakfast: I have coffee. There's this big calendar with lots of stickers to represent the meetings and the horses, and I want to pile as many stickers on each week as I can. No, he'll say, it's not worth running here, or, We've got too many meetings that day as it is. But I don't listen. Stickers mean horses. Horses mean winners. Winners mean champion jockey.

There's a limit to what even the best jockey can do. We can't get a horse to run any faster than its genetic and physiological maximum: what we can do is get it as near to that mark as possible, all the while racing a dozen or more fellow jockeys who are all trying to do the same with their horses. But when the margins between winning and losing are very small, sometimes the difference is down to which jockey controls his horse better. That in turn isn't just a matter of pulling on the reins or using the whip: it's a holistic thing; it's all about the bond I can get with the horse. Some horses

I ride work every week and I know them well, but as often as not, the first time I sit on a horse I'm racing is in the parade ring. So I have five, maybe 10 minutes to form that bond.

A rider's first contact with the horse in the paddock is critical. I make sure my first touch is soft, gentle and respectful, and more often than not the horse responds to that. From the moment I'm on the horse's back I'm using the contact points between me and it – my hands on the reins, my feet in the irons and my arse in the saddle – to let me know how it's feeling and vice versa. A horse isn't a car, where I can just jump aboard, turn the key and set off. Horses sense emotions and feed off them. If I'm positive and relaxed then the horse is more likely to be too – not always, but often. If I'm negative and tight, the horse definitely senses that, and then it becomes negative and tight too, and when that happens I may as well pack up and go home, because no horse wins when it feels like that. There are times when I'm upset after arguing with Dad or Catherine, and as soon as I climb on the horse it knows. It feels what I feel, each and every time.

Every horse is completely different, and each has its own character. Some you have to bully a little and show them who's boss, some you have to encourage, others you have to mollycoddle, and so on. One isn't better than another: it's just the way they are, like people. But it's my job to work out a horse's personality right from the get-go so we've got the best chance of going from A to B quicker than everybody else.

The horse doesn't know how far we're racing, where the turns and the climbs are, or where the winning post is. I do, and I have to impart all that information to him: when to slow, when to speed up, when to run wide, when to tuck in. I think of the horse as a ball of energy which I have to eke out down the length of the course. That energy is like a petrol gauge, and if it's a close race I need it to run out on the line, exactly on the line: not a stride after, and certainly not a stride before.

My dad and Christine come back over to live with me from the end of the all-weather programme in March. I'm not easy to live with, as I put so much pressure on myself to get every winner I possibly can. If I lose, I beat myself up about it. But win or lose, Dad's always on my case: you should have done this, you should have done that, you should have done the other. He's right, of course: he always is. He can read a race better than anyone else I know: he's the one person I can never bullshit. But by the same token he never knows when to leave well alone, never knows that at times less can be more, that I sometimes need bolstering

One of my very first childhood visits to the UK, aged 12.
Here I am on a school trip in sunny Portsmouth.

In the famous St George family silks, aged 25. I used to ride many good horses trained by David Loder for barrister, businessman and racehorse owner Edward St George.

As a teenager on the racetrack in Milan with my dad, Gianfranco. We are by the wonderful San Siro stadium, where I often watched my father ride.

My dad winning the 2000 Guineas at Newmarket on Wollow, who was trained by the famous Sir Henry Cecil, 1976.

At the launch of our new promotional company with Julie Cecil, Walter Swinburn and Lester Piggott, 1993.

Winning the King George and Queen Elizabeth Stakes at Ascot, with the great Lammtarra in 1995. Lammtarra only ran four times in his life and won all four races, including the Prix de l'Arc de Triomphe that year.

Little and large! I'm on a shire horse while Willie Carson is on a miniature pony.
I always enjoyed riding with Willie and deeply admire him as a jockey.

A jockey competition at Santa Anita in Hollywood with (from left to right) Kieren
Fallon, Olivier Peslier, Mick Kinane, Lester Piggott and the great, late Bill Shoemaker.
I used to spend a lot of winters riding there as a teenager to perfect my style.

Winning the King George and Queen Elizabeth Stakes at Ascot on Daylami, 1999.

Receiving the trophy for leading rider at Ascot from Her Majesty the Queen Mother in 1997. How lucky I was to meet her! We jockeys are so fortunate that both the Queen and her mother have had such a passion for our sport.

In Newmarket after Italy won the football World Cup, 2006. What a day that was!

A cold morning on Newmarket Heath with my hero Lester Piggott, 1994.

With Catherine before we were married, a couple of years into our relationship, in 1995. I was proudly sponsored by Alfa Romeo at the time.

Catherine at the equine fertility unit run by her father, Professor Twink Allen.

With our gorgeous baby Leo in 2000.

My family – the true magnificent seven – in 2006.

rather than having every last aspect of my technique and race sense taken to pieces. Often we argue about things for hours late in the evening when I should be getting my sleep in.

When they first came over it was great, as it was just what I needed. A shoulder to cry on, put me back on track, stop the partying. And I know if it weren't for Dad, I wouldn't be who I am today. People often ask whether I'd have been as successful if I'd spent my entire apprenticeship in Italy. I've no doubt about that one. Staying in my own country would not have been a great idea. Because of my dad, life would have been too easy for me, and that's the last thing you need if you want to fight your way to the top. Perhaps my dad sensed this. Yes, I'd have ridden plenty of winners because doors would have been opened for me, but how much further would I have gone? If you are faced with a harsh challenge, self-pride takes over. By sending me away to England, Dad was dropping me in the ocean with a lot of sharks circling. When they first let me loose I was nothing because I was too young to know my limits. Just to prove that I could survive I eventually became bigger than all the other fish. If I'd stayed in Italy I'd have lacked the motivation that being in England provided. Most of all I forced myself to be successful for my father. He was the one I wanted to please above all others, although it was unbelievably difficult in the first few months in Newmarket.

But now I don't need that any more. I'm back on the straight and narrow, I'm champion jockey, I'm with Catherine, but they're still treating me like I'm this wayward kid always about to go off the rails, telling me off for every small thing, never happy with what I do.

I'm asked to go and train Balanchine, this nice filly Godolphin have over in Dubai because they want to enter it in the 1000 Guineas. I don't know the first thing about riding in Dubai. When I first go out there I genuinely think I'll be riding horses on sand dunes, maybe even bareback. But of course when I arrive I see that the facilities are state of the art, absolutely as good as anywhere else: proper racetracks, gallops, trotting rings and so on. When Sheikh Mohammed does something, he does it properly. I meet him and everyone involved in the set-up, and I'm really impressed by everything about them: their ambition, knowledge, professionalism.

Balanchine's a great horse, too. They ask me what I think of her chances. I tell them I think she'll place – finish in the top three – if they run her in the 1000 Guineas.

* * *

We're riding at Lingfield, just another in the endless round of meetings. It's the 4.30, my third race of the afternoon, and so far I've had an eighth place and a second. I'm on the favourite, Aberlady, and until the final three furlongs it's entirely unmemorable. Then suddenly Kalar stumbles and flips his jockey Steve Wood clean off, bouncing him straight into the path of Lift Boy and Moving Image.

Steve doesn't stand a chance. He's hit with shattering force and goes under their hooves. Both those horses go down in the melee. It all happens right in front of me, like watching someone you know being knocked down by a double-decker bus, and immediately I know – as do we all – that he's in a bad way. Tyrone Williams wins on Bells of Longwick, but he doesn't celebrate, and in the weighing room afterwards there's no banter or idle chatter. We're all waiting to hear about Steve's condition.

The news comes, tragic and inevitable: he's died from internal injuries. I'm devastated. He was a good mate and a great lad: we used to call him Samson, as he was so strong, even though he weighed in well under eight stone. He wasn't a superstar, but everybody liked and respected him: he was honest, talented and reliable, and he loved racing with a passion. He had a fiancée and a two-year-old boy.

On the way home I offer up a silent prayer for him, and for them. I'm also thinking exactly the same thoughts that every jockey out there has: there but for the grace of God go I. It's the risk we take every time we get onto a horse's back, and the fact that the chances are low – Steve's the first flat jockey to be killed in a decade – doesn't mean they're non-existent. But if I let myself think about that risk for even a moment, I may as well hang up my irons and go work in a bank. It's an amazing sport, this, and it's given me so much: but sometimes it takes away too, and I have to accept that.

Godolphin put Balanchine straight in to the 1000 Guineas as her first race of the season: no prep race, no nice, easy outing against a lower-class field. John Reid's out in front on Las Meninas, but Balanchine comes like a train at the end and it takes 20 minutes for the judges to study the photo finish and give their verdict: Las Meninas, by a short head.

I'm riding Balanchine in the Oaks. I've been riding winners for seven years now, but have yet to cross the line first in a Classic. This, surely, is my chance. She's only third favourite, but I've got a good feeling about her after the Guineas and am confident that the step up in distance to a mile and a half is just what she wants.

Most jockeys choose to use light nylon gloves to give them more grip on the reins. I make a big mistake, leaving mine in the weighing room. From the moment she jumps out of the stalls, Balanchine pulls so fiercely that the reins are slipping through my hands. Because I can't hold her properly, I have to let her bowl along with the leaders and hope that she keeps going. Luckily it turns out to be the right thing to do. Knowing that when it rains the ground at Epsom is always best nearer the stands, as the camber falls away from there down to the inside rail, I let her stride into the lead running down the hill, so we can ease our way across to that side. Walter Swinburn noses ahead on Hawajiss, and for a few strides I think, *Oh God, I'm going to finish second again*. But the more I ask, the more Balanchine responds. With a furlong to go we're back in front, and then in the last hundred yards we pull right away. Relief floods through me. I've won a Classic. *Finally*.

John and I are flying to France for a Sunday race.

'You look knackered,' he says.

'I am. Absolutely cream crackered.' I pause, not wanting to show weakness – to myself, let alone John – but I sense he'll know how to handle this. 'I'm not sure how much longer I can go on.'

'Then take a break.'

'I'll lose out on winners.'

'Not from racing. From training. Don't worry about riding work for me. I'll get the stable lads to cover for you. Catch up on your sleep, refuel your tank, get your mojo back.'

It's just what I want to hear. John understands what I need off the horse as well as on it. I count myself lucky to have not just such a good trainer, but such a good man too in my corner.

Because it's tiring, racing. Maybe it doesn't look that tiring compared to running or cycling or swimming, but it is, trust me. It's not just the physical effort of controlling horse after horse – sometimes I can ride a dozen in a day – when you haven't eaten enough, but it's also the mental strain: the tension, the intensity, the pressure, the attention to detail and the anticipation. And then, of course, you have the fact that so many people are invested not just emotionally but financially too: I win and lose people money every day, so I kind of feel responsible. I don't put a gun to people's heads and make them go and bet on my horse, of course, but even so, it's quite a pressure to have.

It's a treadmill, and it never stops. You get on a horse, you ride, you win, you lose. Half an hour later you get on another horse, you ride, you win, you lose. Half an hour after that … It's brutal. It's the only job where you go to work and you're followed by an ambulance. In football if you get injured then you rest. In racing if you get injured then you strap yourself back on the next horse. Jockeys get battered. We never stop.

It's all I can do to keep on that treadmill. The winners and the losers come along, and I haven't got time to enjoy it: it's always onto the next race. No time to enjoy the highs, no time to sulk about the lows. I can't afford to take even a step out, because then it's very hard to get back in. I just have to keep the revs up and keep on going. Why do I keep going? Because it's a drug. I'm riding this beautiful animal at 40 mph, I'm competing with another 12, 14, 16 riders and horses, we're all racing to within half an inch of each other. The competition, the adrenaline, the crowd, the smell. That's why I do it. And then on top of that, if I win, the jubilation, the excitement, the thrill, the applause, the stage. That's why I do it. It's all of that in a package.

I've got a runner for the Queen every day at Royal Ascot. On the first day of the festival I'm told there's someone to see me. I go out of the weighing room and look up, and up, and up. It's a massive guy in tails and a top hat, and he's so tall that I find myself looking all the way up his nose and thinking how hairy it is.

'Carnarvon,' he says.

I know who he is now: Lord Carnarvon, the Queen's racing manager.

'Do you know how to address the Queen, boy?' *Not a Scooby-Doo*, I think, but before I can answer he ploughs on. 'You touch your hat, you bow, you say, "Your Majesty". If she asks you a question you reply and end your sentence with the word "ma'am", to rhyme with "ham" not "harm". If she doesn't ask you a question then you say nothing.'

Later the Queen turns up, and I remember what to do: touch the hat, make a bow, say, 'Your Majesty.'

She asks me what the going's like, and I reply, 'Good to firm, ma'am.'

Nailed it.

The next day she asks about tactics. By Friday we're having a proper conversation and I'm feeling a bit more comfortable. On Saturday morning, however, there's not a soul in sight. The racecourse seems empty after the huge crowds of the previous days, and even though I'm riding her filly Zenith in the opening race, it never occurs to me that the Queen will be there to watch: Zenith's not exactly the next Miesque, put it that way.

There's not a soul around as I wander into the paddock, chatting away to jockeys on each side of me, just the usual rubbish about cars and girls. Suddenly they go quiet. I look round and there's the Queen, two paces in front of me. I freeze, not knowing what to say.

I frantically touch my cap, give a comical bow and blurt out, 'Ow are ya?' in a Cockney accent to shame Dick Van Dyke. Lord Carnarvon kicks me as though he's an Italian defender and I'm clean through on goal, but the Queen just smiles, opens her arms and replies, 'I'm still here.'

On 11 June I'd reached three figures, aptly enough for John at York on Winter Coat. Last year I'd managed fewer than 20 at the same stage of the season. I don't know that much about cricket, but I do know that once they score a ton the best batsmen start all over again and press on remorselessly towards a double century. That's exactly my plan too: keep my head down, try to maintain the winning run and hope that nothing goes wrong.

And that's more or less what happens. The double ton comes with a treble at York on 1 September, the quickest that landmark's ever been reached. Some people are even talking about me going on to break one of the greatest records of them all, Sir Gordon Richards's 269 winners in 1947. But by now I'm running on empty, exponentially more knackered than I was when John gave me a short break back in May, and again he comes to the rescue. He knows that a jockey as exhausted as I am could be an actual hazard, to myself and to my competitors.

'Ease up these last few weeks,' he says. 'You've won the championship, and Sir Gordon's record is probably out of reach anyway no matter what you do.'

There is one record I want to pass before the end of the season, however, and that belongs to my old man. He rode 229 in his best season. I get to 233 and I'm finished. I've been on the go for 10 months more or less non-stop, and I can hardly get up to bed at night or out of bed in the morning. I've ridden 1,300 races this year, seven days out of seven, week in, week out. I'm cooked. The last few weeks especially I've just been grinding it out, no joy in what I'm doing. It's just numbers, and though I've set my heart on this and I'm glad I'm winning, I'm not the kind of guy who's ever been just about the numbers, that's not me.

Dad's not happy. You can still win more, he says. This race here, that race: they're yours to win.

I tell him he's not listening to me. I'm done, I say. I beat your record, I stepped out from your shadow for once. I've had enough and I'm fried. If you're not happy then that's not my problem, because I'm happy. If you're not happy then go back to Italy.

In fact, I'd like you to go back, because having you here is no longer helping me.

He and Christine go back to Italy. The house is very quiet without them: not just an absence of sound but a silence almost like a force in itself.

I don't speak to him for a year.

Being with Catherine changes me. Gradually I realise how selfish I've been about my career. That doesn't change totally – perhaps she would say it doesn't change all that much! – because you have to be selfish if you're to stay at the top of your game in such a competitive arena, but at least I become aware of it and try to dial it back when I can. A relationship is give and take, and you can't just take all the time. So I have to readjust myself. She also helps teach me to see the bigger picture and to find that balance I've been looking for, so that it's not all or nothing. She shows me that it doesn't have to be all racing 24/7 or all partying: that I can have a mix. Like normal people do, I guess. Before I was with her, there were three people I felt were important: me, myself and I. Now it's two, her and me.

She deals with my moods too. Everybody says I'm up and down. I can't really judge myself on this front because I feel that I'm normal, but everyone thinks that about themselves, I guess. Anyway, everyone says I'm up and down, and they can't all be wrong. When I'm happy I bounce around and I want the world to love life the way I do; when I'm down I'm a grumpy bugger and I guess that infects the mood of those around me too. Thing is, neither of these extremes last very long, not unless there's something really wrong (or really right) in my life. It's like clouds on a sunny day: they might pass over the sun and make things a little darker and chillier for a while, but not for that long.

It's late October. I'm pretty much fully rested when Luca rings me out of the blue and asks me to come and ride work on Barathea, who's won the Queen Anne Stakes this year and triumphed in last year's Irish 2000 Guineas.

When I get to Luca's yard I see what he has in mind, and instantly I'm excited: he's built a tight, left-handed bend, just like the one at Churchill Downs where the Breeders' Cup is taking place next month. He wants to see how Barathea will handle the course.

I leap on board, trot up to the start and ask Barathea to give me all he's got. The turn is sharp, but he takes it like a greyhound. Every piece of work he does after that is top quality, absolutely gleaming. It's almost as though he knows what we've got in mind for him.

The day before he's due to be loaded on the plane, I

give Barathea his final pre-race run out. Luca watches us all the way.

'Think he's going to win?' he says when I dismount.

'No,' I reply. 'I *know* he's going to win.'

The Breeders' Cup is huge. It takes place at a different racecourse in the US every year, and there are 14 races sorted by category, with prize money in the millions. For me, the Breeders' Cup is like the Ryder Cup: it's Europe against America. I feel very strongly that when I go there I'm not just riding for me, the trainers and the owners: I'm riding for Europe, to show that our way of doing things is just as good as theirs. You know what the Americans are like: they big themselves up, they're keen to kick us when we're down, and the competitor in me gets an extra sense of fight, gets really aggressive. What makes me tick is that it's in their backyard. It's all stacked in their favour: their tracks, their crowds; we've got transport for horses and jet lag for riders, and so on. So if I win there it's very much been against the odds.

All day before the race I repeat to myself the simplest and most important mantra: *get out fast*. It's not that I want to lead, but I do want to be able to pick my spot just behind the leaders, the sweet spot where I can cover any move without making Barathea expend too much energy.

Get out fast. Get out fast.

That's just what we do. Barathea jumps out like a star-tled cat, putting us ahead of the rush for position. I'm where I want to be, travelling like a dream. Round the bend and into the straight, Barathea's cruising on auto-pilot, the only one still on the bridle. It's a heady feeling, knowing he's the strongest in the race and all I need to do is time the final kick right for maximum effect. Two furlongs out I could go if I want to, but there's no other horse getting away from us just yet, so why risk even the slightest chance of him blowing up? I wait, and wait, and wait … and at the furlong pole I tell him to go.

He puts on the afterburners. Some horses need a few strides to get up to full pace. Not Barathea. His change of pace is instant: one click of the fingers, bang! and he's gone.

That last furlong is magic. It's not just the sense of knowing I've won a massive race, or striking a blow for English horses out here, or even that this win will put me on the map in America. It's also payback for Luca, a final restoration of our relationship. He rushes out to greet us, and I'm so excited that I lean down and plant a massive smacker on his cheek.

'I'm going to do a flying dismount,' I say as we're led back to the winner's enclosure.

'Are you sure?'

'I've been wanting to do it for years.' And I've always been put off by how much the stuffy old British racing establishment will disapprove of it. But this is Kentucky, where they love a showman.

'What if you break your leg?'

'Who cares? It'll heal before next season.'

This is why I practised those dismounts so often on those winter trips to Santa Anita. I slip my toes out of the irons, bend my knees and launch myself skywards before landing nimbly on both feet beside Barathea. It might not earn maximum points for artistic impression, but at least I don't fall on my face. The crowd roar with delight. It's party time!

When I get back home I see that the racing papers are full of letters from people complaining about my flying dismount. The hell with them. This kind of stuff can get to me if I let it. I read the papers and they're full of criticism, half of it from people who wouldn't know which end the horse shits from, and I'm like, just fuck off, you know? I know when I've ridden badly, and I don't need a journalist to tell me. It's like any sport: there are those who know what they're looking at and those who don't. I know who's in the first category, and it's those people whose opinion I seek out and respect.

* * *

There's an old saying in sport: the only thing harder than getting to the top is staying there. I don't want 1994 to be seen as a flash in the pan, a one-time triumph never to be repeated. So I'm just as determined to retain my champion jockey title as I was to win it in the first place, which means another couple of months on the all-weather.

This time, however, I don't have it all my own way. Jason Weaver matches me stride for stride through the worst of the winter in January and February, and our long friendship becomes strained to the limit once he heads the table for the first time.

Until now we've always travelled to the races together whenever possible. Not any more. Not now we're at each other's throats. He wasn't a dick to me last year when I was out in front, but I'm not gracious or mature enough to return the compliment. I'm a horrible little bastard to him, and all because I want to win so badly.

The simmering resentment between us is bound to come to a head sooner or later, and at Lingfield on 16 March it does. I try to make all the running on the favourite Nordico Express, and with two furlongs left, Jason comes alongside on Dolly Face. We race head to head and toe to toe, cursing and shouting, whips banging, the pair of us going for it as though we are fighting out the finish of the Derby rather than a Mickey Mouse event in front of a deserted grandstand. I think I've just done enough, but Dolly Face nails us right on the line. Jason yells his triumph to the heavens before turning round and raising his hand for me to give him a high five. What I give him instead is a torrent of abuse. It's not something I'm proud of, but in the heat of the moment I just can't help myself.

This is my fourth Derby, and I'm on a good horse: Tamure, fourth favourite at 9/1. We settle in well and turn for home in third place, with Richard Hills out in front on Fahal. Richard kicks for home and I go after him, but the gap's only closing very slowly. *Go on*, I urge Tamure, *go on*. He's straining all he can, but Fahal's coming back to us almost in slow motion, and for a moment I wonder whether we'll run out of racetrack, as we're well within the final furlong now.

A hundred yards from home, and finally – *finally* – I get Tamure's nose in front of Fahal. Richard's still urging Fahal on, but I know now that we have them, and I sense Fahal beginning to fall back. The crowd noise is like a tsunami at my back and all around me.

I'm going to win the Derby. This race I've dreamed about winning for the past 15 years, this race for which my dad said he'd give me his most prized watch, this race … I'm going to win it.

I have this feeling for a second, maximum. Then Walter Swinburn, riding Lammtarra, comes past on the outside like a steam train. One moment he's just a shadow at the corner of my eye, the next I'm looking at Lammtarra's hindquarters a length down. We hold on for second, but it's not much consolation. For that brief moment in time I held the prize in my hands, so close I could practically touch it, taste it, smell it. Then it was gone.

I wonder if I'll ever get such a good chance again.

It's July, I'm back out in front in the Jockeys Championship, and since I'm suspended for a few days I'm at my dad's home in Sardinia – we are finally speaking again. Mattie rings.

'Are you sitting down?' he asks.

'Yes.'

'You're riding Lammtarra in the King George at the end of the week.'

'No way!'

'Gospel truth.'

It's not just that until now I didn't have a ride in the race: it's also that I'd presumed Walter would be riding Lammtarra, as he'd won the Derby on him. I don't exactly know why he's not – there are rumours of arguments between him and the trainer Saeed bin Suroor, who works for Sheikh Mohammed's brother Sheikh Maktoum – but to be honest, I don't try that hard to find out, because I don't really care. This kind of thing happens all the time in racing, and we jockeys very rarely have anything to do with it. We just ride for whoever wants us. All I care about is that I've got the ride, and since I didn't go looking for it, I know that Walter can't have any beef with me personally: and indeed he doesn't. He tells me everything I need to know about Lammtarra, whom I've never even sat on.

'He'll keep finding more in the finish,' he says. 'Remember that, Frankie. Whatever you give him, he can take it. He's a hell of a horse.'

I appreciate Walter's kindness and honesty, but I also know that only a win will do, otherwise the press will be all over me as the man who screwed up the King George.

As we approach the final bend I'm pumping away furiously without any immediate response. Turning for home we're flat out, the race coming nicely to the boil. Michael Hills comes past absolutely swinging on the bridle on Pentire, and to the crowd it might look all over, but I know better.

He'll keep finding more in the finish.

Lammtarra loves a proper scrap. For the next two furlongs we have a right old ding-dong. Pentire's just ahead, but Lammtarra keeps coming, and coming, and coming. Michael is asking Pentire for more, just as I am of Lammtarra, but only one horse has still got something left.

Whatever you give him, he can take it.

We flash past the post a neck ahead, and I've got shivers down my spine.

'Best ride I've ever seen you do,' Sheikh Mohammed says to me afterwards. I'm flattered, but I also suspect that Lammtarra's courage flattered me a bit.

Apart from being champion jockey, there are three other things I want from this season: to get to the 1,000 career winners mark, to win the St Leger so I can wear the floppy velvet cap which by tradition is always presented to the successful jockey, and to win the Arc, which is, along with the Derby, the most prestigious race in Europe.

The first two come at exactly the same time, a perfect coincidence that couldn't be scripted. I'm on Classic Cliche, who many think is past it but whose chances I fancy: he keeps on going all the way to the end each and every time he races, and I'm confident he's going to stay the distance of one and three-quarter miles. He's a massive, powerful animal, like a giant charger, and I hope that once he gets into a rhythm he'll be hard to pass. That's exactly what happens, though the other jockeys must think I'm crazy when I kick him into a clear lead with well over three furlongs left. He keeps going strongly right to the line and could hardly win more easily, though I dare not look round until the last 50 yards.

I never get used to losing, and I certainly never enjoy it or just shrug it off. I don't think there is such a thing as a good loser in top-flight racing, or indeed in any other sport. When it's your livelihood rather than your hobby: well, show me a good loser and I'll show you a loser. If that's your attitude then just go and do a nine-to-five job.

But I do get better at accepting it. Even the best jockey loses way, way more often than he wins: I win one in every five or six, for example, and that's better than almost anyone else. So those four or five that I lose, if I kill myself for them every time, then I won't be alive. So I put up with it. It's hard to swallow, but I try to use the losses to make a winner more likely next time out: to learn from my mistakes, keep my resolve high and make the one winner count for just that little bit more in my head than the four or five losers. That winner is always going to pull me back up: there's always a little bit of light at the end of the tunnel, because if it's doom and gloom all the time then I wouldn't do it. I'd think, *What's the point?*

And of course out there on the track it's just me on my own, no teammates, so I have to accept it on my own. The only ones who really understand how it feels are my fellow jockeys, and we don't really talk about it. No one else understands, not really.

Now all my thoughts turn to the Arc in Paris. I've got two possible rides, Balanchine and Lammtarra.

'Which one are you leaning towards?' asks Simon Crisford, Sheikh Mohammed's racing manager.

'Balanchine, I think.'

Simon raises an eyebrow. He rings Sheikh Mohammed and puts him on speakerphone.

'Frankie rides Lammtarra,' says Sheikh Mohammed.

The phone goes dead.

'I guess that settles it,' Simon says.

For weeks Dad's been drumming into my head the importance of a sharp start in the Arc. We must have spoken a hundred times. The only thing that matters, he says over and again, is to jump out smartly like a sprinter, go flat out and get in the first three. Remember the Breeders' Cup last year? Different course, different horse, same tactic.

Lammtarra jumps off so well that I can settle him in the ideal spot: second place, three or four lengths behind Luso, who gives us a perfect tow. At the top of the straight, aware that the challenges will soon be coming from all directions, I know it's time to go. Three furlongs out: go early, seize first run, ride the sting out of our rivals. Lammtarra responds like a champion, pouncing on Luso and heading for home at full power. The crowd noise is deafening, as it always is at the Arc.

It's a cloudy day and I'm wearing dark goggles, so everything seems remote, dream-like. Lammtarra and I are in a world of our own: all in slow motion, just like the movies. Challengers appear and fall back one by one, unable to live with the white heat of Lammtarra's pace: but now comes Olivier Peslier on Freedom Cry up the middle, and they're not fading.

Come on, boy. Find me just that little bit more, like Walter said you would.

It's as though Lammtarra digs into some reserve tank of fuel, a last little boost – and we draw away from Freedom Cry and cross the line in front.

I end the season as champion again, on 217 winners, the first jockey since Sir Gordon in 1952 to claim back-to-back double centuries. Again, people ask whether I'll have a tilt at his fabled 269, but I'm not going to for three reasons. First, the rules are changing back so that winter winners on the all-weather circuits will no longer count towards the title. Second, Godolphin's rapid expansion means they need me more and more overseas. Finally, riding flat out for 10 months is just too exhausting. At least I have solid external reasons for not taking it on in 1996. Besides, I've proved myself to everyone who doubted, and then some. In two years I've ridden 2,300 races and won 450 of them. That's enough.

John rings me. The moment he speaks, I know he's got bad news: his voice sounds so shaken.

'Chuck was killed in a car crash this morning,' he says simply.

Chuck was Barney Curley's son, barely old enough to have passed his driving test. Of all the people for this tragedy to befall, it seems so unfathomably cruel that it has to be Barney.

It's the first funeral I've ever been to. I help carry the coffin out of the church. Chuck's girlfriend is there – it's her sixteenth birthday today, like this is some sort of sick cosmic joke.

At the wake I talk to Neil Foreman, who flies a small plane and often takes me and Barney from course to course. Barney and Neil are usually taking the piss out of each other non-stop. But today Barney just looks blankly at Neil, says, 'There's no joking now.'

The start of the 1996 season sees a subtle change in my job description. Whereas before my relationship with Godolphin was close but still fundamentally informal, now I'm officially their stable jockey and number one rider. They have first claim on me whenever they have a runner in a race. In return I get a handsome retainer, a Mercedes which is replaced every so often, and three months in Dubai over the winter: training in the dawn sunshine, topping up my tan in the afternoon, and thanking my lucky stars I'm not flogging my guts out in the depths of a Fenland winter.

Catherine and I have been together for two and a half years, and I know she's the woman I want to marry. On Valentine's Day, back in London for a few days, I take her to lunch at Scalini, my favourite Italian restaurant, just behind Harrods. I've got an engagement ring burning a hole in my pocket, but somehow I keep it together till after the main course.

'Put your napkin over your eyes,' I say.

'Don't be daft.'

'Well then, please at least turn away.'

'Frankie, why are you behaving so weirdly?'

'Please. Just turn away for a moment.'

She does so, if only to humour someone who's clearly taken leave of his senses.

I drop onto one knee and take her hands in mine. 'Catherine Allen, will you marry me?'

She says yes, which is lucky as I don't really have a Plan B. The waiters start clapping, and within seconds the entire restaurant has joined in.

The highlight of my time in Dubai is the first Dubai World Cup, a meeting designed to put the emirate on the map of world racing. There's a huge party in the desert with thousands of guests, and a private Simply Red concert at the Hilton Beach Club, with the waves lapping on the shore only yards from the stage. Naomi Campbell's there, plus some of the cast from *Baywatch*. You don't get any of this at Wolverhampton on a Tuesday evening, that's for sure.

Walter normally sits next to me in the weighing room, but not at the moment. Riding in Hong Kong in our off-season, a horse called Liffey River catapulted him into the running rail, breaking his shoulder blade, collarbone and ribs, puncturing a lung and causing serious blood loss. Doctors said that if he'd taken even 15 more minutes to get to hospital he'd have died, and even as it was he was in a coma for four days. Coming only 18 months after Samson's death, it's another reminder that danger is always out there, stalking the tracks for when we least expect it.

Walter's peg is empty for month after month. I miss him: his chat, his eccentricities, his advice. When he's here I watch him like a hawk, trying to pick up his best attributes. He's such a natural talent, a great horseman. The place isn't the same without him.

At Newbury I'm riding a highly strung grey filly called Shawanni for Godolphin. She's a great big horse with a nasty side to her, one of those animals who just spells trouble, and today she's in a particularly vile mood. The moment I jump on her back in the paddock, she freezes and won't move. I quickly slip my feet out of the irons and ask her lad to take a half-turn behind some of the other horses, as she doesn't seem to appreciate being out in front on her own. She takes a couple of steps and freezes again.

Fear clutches me hard and fast, because when fillies freeze like this they mean to somersault backwards and squash you. If my feet were still in the stirrups I might be able to thrust away from her before impact, but now I've got no means of escape. She's going to break my pelvis if I don't do something. I twist as I fall and land on my left elbow. The pain is searing and immediate, and I know instantly that I've smashed my elbow.

Jane Chapple-Hyam, Peter's wife, is first to my side and asks for the pin on my collar to be removed to assist my breathing. The medics arrive and take a look at me.

'Bad bruising here,' one of them says.

'I've shattered my elbow,' I reply, and even the effort of speaking hurts like fury.

I'm taken to hospital, but the casualty department is overrun and it's an hour and a half before I'm taken down to X-ray. By now I'm in bits. The pain is unbelievable. The X-ray shows that the bone from my upper arm has been forced right through my elbow joint. They give me a pain-killing injection and wheel me into a private ward.

The surgeon Richard Dodds operates on me the next morning.

'How long till I'm back in action?' I ask.

'Four to six months.'

I do what I always do in these situations: take the most optimistic timeframe and halve it. Only two months out, if I work hard at it. Four to six months is for normal people not used to hard physical work and with no real incentive to go through the pain barrier. So I start working like fury on the rehab as soon as I can, because I want to salvage something from the season.

Watching Royal Ascot at home on TV is a grim experience. So many of the horses I expected to be riding run well, starting with Charnwood Forest, who takes the opening race on Tuesday. After missing three more winners on the Thursday – including Classic Cliche in the Gold Cup – I'm like a bear with a sore head, making everyone around me miserable.

I have to get out of the house. So on the spur of the moment on Friday I decide to go to Ascot for the final day. I borrow a morning suit from Bruce Raymond, cut off an arm from one of my shirts, and hitch a ride with John and Rachel Gosden. I go into the weighing room and chat to the jockeys, but it's a little strange being there when I'm not riding. Everyone's in a rush: not unfriendly, but definitely preoccupied. For the first time I see it as an outsider must do, and I don't like the feeling: I want to be back with my tribe.

One of John's newer owners is Ronnie Wood, who's thrilled to meet me – the feeling is very mutual, trust me – and is keener on racing than almost anyone I've ever met. I want to ask him about life with The Stones and all his tales of rock 'n' roll excess, but he only wants to talk about horses!

Sheikh Mohammed tells me he's retired Shawanni. The first time she was ridden after Newbury she dived under a running rail on the gallops at Newmarket with her lad still on her back. It's the right decision, the only possible decision. Sooner or later she'd have killed someone, it's as simple as that.

I start rehab as soon as possible. However long you wait, it always hurts at first. Once the bone has healed in four weeks or so you have to get it moving. Of course it hurts: the limb is rusty and all the muscles and ligaments are slack. You just have to go through the pain barrier. That's the part that people don't understand. It's true that all injured jocks come back too early, but in such a competitive sport we have no choice.

I'm back in time to ride Shantou in the St Leger for John. Faintly absurdly for such a brilliant trainer, he's yet to win a Classic, and the press are giving him plenty of grief. Outwardly he seems unaffected, because that's how he seems about everything, but I know how much it hurts inside. I want to retain my St Leger crown from last year, but I want to do it at least as much for John as for myself. He put his faith in me when others hesitated, and I never forget that.

Shantou's a right old bruiser who knows to handle himself. Just as at Epsom three months earlier, we end up in a sustained scrap with Pat Eddery on Dushyantor. Dushyantor cruises into the lead two furlongs out, but Shantou's not done yet. We lock horns and go at it like two street fighters trading punches, both looking for the knockout blow. Aware that Dushyantor rides best when responding to a challenge up close and personal, I let Shantou drift right-handed away from him into the centre of the course before giving him three or four quick cracks with my whip in the last 50 yards. He lunges forward and in the last 10 strides inches ahead to win.

When John walks up to the podium to collect his trophy, my vision is swimming from the tears of pride in my eyes.

I've got a few days off, so I go to Henlow Grange, a health farm, with Catherine. In between all the mud baths and massages, one of the women doing the treatments asks when my next big meeting is.

'I've got seven at Ascot on Saturday,' I reply.

'Any tips?'

'To be honest, your best bet isn't any of those, but my first one the next day: Sunbeam Dance in the 2.00 – 7/2 favourite but still good odds even at that price. Cracking horse.'

'So I shouldn't put any on for the Saturday?'

'Nah. Sunbeam Dance's your best bet.'

'OK, thanks.'

'Mind you,' I add, 'you know what they say?'

'What do they say?'

'Never take advice from a jockey. We're the worst tipsters in the world.'

3

ASCOT

Sometimes the things which change your life come out of a clear blue sky.

Yesterday I rode six at Haydock with nothing to show for it except a lousy journey home on a Friday night. This morning I study the form for today's races, as I always do. I'm riding seven at Ascot this afternoon, and I go down the card one by one.

The first race I should win.

The second one, no chance: it's way too tough.

The third race, the Queen Elizabeth Stakes, is the most important of the lot, and that's a two-horse contest between Pat and me: I'll stalk him for much of the race and then try to outdo him for turn of foot in the closing stages.

The fourth is an impossibility: my draw's a difficult one and the horse is not good enough to compensate for that.

The fifth is unlikely.

The sixth is a reprise of the third, a two-horse race between Pat and me.

And the seventh is a total impossibility, more so than two and four combined: the horse hasn't won for a year and is carrying a stone more than usual.

So seven races, and three possible wins at best. To be honest, I'd be happy just to win race three, the QE2: this and the Ascot Gold Cup are the only trophies the Queen presents in person, and this was also the very first Group 1 race I won six years ago on Markofdistinction.

Just another day at the races. Just the day that will change my life for ever.

There's always a special atmosphere at Ascot when the Queen's there. I feel this atmosphere, smell it, respond to it. I'm getting pumped up and nervous.

First up is Wall Street in the Cumberland Lodge Stakes. Wall Street has plenty of stamina so I plan to sit close behind the obvious danger, Salmon Ladder, then press for home once we hit the straight. It's a bit of a surprise to find myself in front after a few strides, but Wall Street seems happy making the running at a sound pace so I let him bowl along before quickening it up on the home turn. Salmon Ladder presses us hard over the last two furlongs, but Wall Street keeps pulling out more and wins well by half a length. It's the perfect start, and if nothing else it's nice to get a winner early so I know the day won't be a complete washout.

Race two, Diffident in the Diadem Stakes over six furlongs, is a big field, hence my pessimism about my chances. 'Sam,' I say to Godolphin's travelling head lad Sam Avis, 'if we win this I'll bare my bum under Newmarket's clock tower.' On Diffident's previous outing, at Newmarket, he was far too keen and ran a stinker. He's one of those frustrating horses that have lots of speed but refuse to settle. Inconsistent would be a better name for him. Infuriating, perhaps.

I drop him in close behind the leading bunch as Averti takes us along at a smart gallop. Diffident half-settles for me, and it probably helps that the horses in front of us are weaving around, blocking our path. Nine times out of 10 this race would play out like nothing special: I'd be in the middle of the pack all the way round, not good enough to win but not bad enough to be shelled out the back. But this is the tenth time, when things just fall into place.

I try to edge past on the left, but the door's closed on me before I can get through. I switch to the right and try to squeeze through there, and again I'm blocked off. I'm running out of time and track, but now a gap opens up on the left and I get first run on Walter and Lucayan

Prince to go after the leader, Leap for Joy. When sprinters are jostling for position, races are won and lost in a split second. Diffident gets in front of Leap for Joy right on the line, but Lucayan Prince is there too and we three cross the line in as close a triple dead-heat as you're ever likely to see. The photo confirms it: Diffident by a short head from Lucayan Prince, with Leap for Joy another short head back in third. It couldn't have been any closer. I should never have won that: I got lucky – it happens.

Now it's race three: the big one, the Queen Elizabeth. Pat's on Bosra Sham, a great filly trained by Henry Cecil; I'm on Mark of Esteem. There's a backstory to this one too: Henry trained Mark of Esteem as a two-year-old before he and Sheikh Mohammed fell out, so now Henry's hoping that Bosra Sham will give him a victory which won't just be revenge in itself, but could also seal the trainers' championship over Saeed bin Suroor. There's so much at stake and the tension's ratcheted right up, not just for me but for everybody.

The Sheikh has total faith in Mark of Esteem. The horse's top speed is phenomenal, but I doubt he can sustain it for more than a furlong, and Sheikh Mohammed is evidently of the same mind. He gives me final instructions in the paddock: 'Wait. Wait again. Wait even longer. Then reach for the rocket booster.'

I stalk Bosra Sham the whole way, biding my time. Some horses can go from three furlongs out, and Mark of Esteem's not one of them, so I have to keep my finger on the trigger without ever pressing it. *Wait. Wait again. Wait even longer.* A furlong out, Michael Kinane appears on my outside on our stable companion Charnwood Forest, just as I'm about to make my move, but he lets me out and I'm through. *Reach for the rocket booster.* Mark of Esteem just flies, absolutely flies: like a cat, crouched, athletic and low to the ground, almost knocking me out of the saddle as we catapult into the clear. I punch the air as I cross the line and salute the crowd. I've never had a feeling quite like it in my life: that's the best performance of any miler I've ridden. He was lined up against a tip-top field, and he slaughtered them. On the way back to unsaddle I'm uncontainable. My first three rides have yielded victories in a Group 3, a Group 2 and now a Group 1 race, all for the team that retains me. If ever there's a perfect excuse for a flying dismount, this is it – but as if reading my thoughts, an official walking alongside warns me not to do it.

I reach the winner's enclosure. Sheikh Mohammed calls out: 'Go on, Frankie! Jump!' So I do.

The Queen gives me the trophy, and this time I manage not to sound like Dick Van Dyke when I talk to her. I'm on cloud nine, the crowd cheering and the photographers snapping away. I've won the big race, the one I came here for, so as far as I'm concerned it's job done: anything else from here on in is just a bonus.

There's never much time to waste at these meetings, and we're not even halfway through the card. I run into the weighing room, get a new set of silks on, and now it's race four. I'm on Decorated Hero, known affectionately in John's yard as Square Wheels because he's such a bad mover. The field for the Tote Festival Handicap is massive – 26 runners – and since I have to come across from stall 22, I figure I'll lose too much ground and it won't happen for me. I do lose a lot of ground, but only because they all go off like the clappers: way too fast, a totally unsustainable pace. I decide to do my own thing, and we're so far back early on that we're dead last. I gradually ease Decorated Hero all the way over to the stands rails and creep into the race. The horses in front are looking a bit tired as we move stealthily into the action with two furlongs left. One by one they all fade and die in front of me, and one by one I pick them off. When I launch Decorated Hero on a powerful late run he sweeps to the front a furlong out and finishes so well that he's three and a half lengths clear by the line. I can't remember the last time a race was handed to me on a plate like this.

To be honest, I'm still buzzing from the Queen Elizabeth, so this victory passes me by a bit, at least in emotional terms. Not so the crowd. I'm four from four now, and the atmosphere's changing. Sometimes there's a lull after the big race, but my winning streak means that's not the case here. The crowd sense it almost earlier than I do: something special might be happening.

Now I've got four in the bag and am back in the royal blue colours of Godolphin on Fatefully, a red-hot favourite in the mile handicap. She's well drawn in stall six over the straight mile and I think she has a decent chance of being placed, but 7/4 seems a ridiculous price in such a tight race with 18 runners – until, that is, I realise the skinny odds are being created by the sheer weight of money rolling forward from multiple bets on my mounts.

Once again I get lucky. As the field bunch near the stands rails soon after halfway, I'm trapped behind a wall of horses. I search desperately for a bit of daylight: not much, just enough to squeeze through. Finally I get it, and I have to go for it before it disappears. I kick Fatefully forward, and I hear Jason Weaver on Ninia shout, 'Go on, Frankie, go get 'em!' As we squeeze through Fatefully drifts a little left, causing Pat to check on Questonia as they drop back. We hit the front on the rails with just over a furlong to run, and then Ray

Cochrane on Abeyr comes with a furious late run on the outside. For a moment I think they're going to pip us on the line, but we hold on by a whisker. The stewards hold an inquiry into the contact between Fatefully and Questonia, but I don't think anything will come of it, and indeed it doesn't. They conclude that the interference was accidental, and Pat helps by telling them that his filly was beaten at the time the two horses touched.

Five in a row, on a Saturday, at Ascot, on TV. If ever there was a time and place to do it, it's here. I can tell this is something – something that's not quite usual. This is some mystery power that's making me do this, because I'm not fully in control of what's happening. It's just natural instinct and adrenaline taking over.

I go back to the changing room and get ready for race six, the Blue Seal Conditions Stakes. I'm sitting on the bench, putting my hat on, and suddenly I have a quick – well, it's almost a panic attack. My palms are sweaty, my breath shallow, my mouth dry: because I know that in 350 years of racing only Sir Gordon Richards, Alec Russell and Willie Carson have won six in a row on one day. Imagine joining that list: imagine keeping that kind of company. Equalling that record would be amazing.

In the paddock Ian Balding's looking worried, wondering if I've used up all my magic. 'Lochangel's so fast she might not last six furlongs on a stiff track like this,' he says. 'Be patient, drop her in behind the leaders and give her every chance to stay the distance.'

That's easier said than done in a field of only five runners. Lochangel's both strong and keen, so when she jumps out of the stalls in front it makes sense to let her run. Nobody's taking me on, so I think, *Sod it, I'll let her bowl. Why take her back and forfeit an early advantage?* So much for my orders. As Lochangel sails along eagerly in the lead I try to save a bit, aware that she might hit a brick wall towards the end.

Three hundred metres to go. I ask her to quicken up. We're still out in the clear on our own. Where's Pat, on Corsini? I keep expecting them to appear at any moment, but by the time they finally do it's all too late and Lochangel holds on cosily by three-quarters of a length. I punch the air again when I win, and that's it. Six! Record equalled! I can't believe it.

Pat's fuming as we walk back together. He feels the instructions he was given to drop Corsini in during the first part of the race hindered him, and he thinks he could have beaten us left to his own devices. I sympathise – it's not unusual for trainers and jockeys to disagree on tactics, and whenever that comes before a loss the blame game always starts – but to be honest it's all I can do to keep up with the attention on me.

All hell breaks loose as we return to unsaddle. I come back into the winner's enclosure, and everyone's applauding. They give me a bottle of champagne, and I spray everyone. I'm pushed and pulled in all directions for interviews and presentations. 'Don't touch me!' I bark at the BBC's Julian Wilson. 'I'm red-hot! I'm on fire!'

But there's also a race seven, right? So I go back into the changing room and get ready for it, and now I've got everybody behind me. Come on, Frankie, come on. You can do it. Seven out of seven, the magnificent seven, lucky number seven. And silly as it might sound, this is literally the first time I've even thought about this race, as Fujiyama Crest is a 14/1 shot. No disrespect, but I've got as much chance on a shopping trolley as I have on him. Yes, he won the same race – the Gordon Carter Handicap – with me 12 months earlier as a progressive three-year-old, but that was his last victory. He's been running like a dog all season and has shot up in the weights: the handicapper has him by the throat, and this time the task must be way beyond him. Even at his best he's an awkward thing to ride: a bit like a dinosaur, tall and narrow with a big, long neck.

I don't want this race to spoil my day. In normal circumstances I wouldn't think twice about it, so why change that now? It's still the same race. Whatever the result, I really don't care, because it won't take away the six wins I've had already.

I have to fight my way through the crowd to get to the parade ring. They're all cheering and telling me I can do it, and so is Walter. He's pumping me up as we walk: 'Come on, this is yours, this is your day. You're going to win all seven. Concentrate. Pull your finger out.'

'You're mad, Wally,' I reply. 'That fall you had in Hong Kong's made you soft in the head. Wake up here, get real. Just look at the form book and you'll see why you're wasting your breath.'

We pass the bookies' stalls: 2/1 favourite, they're offering. I blink and look twice, convinced that I've misread it: 12/1, sure; 2/1? That's *insane*.

But 2/1 it is. Everyone in the place is backing me.

In the paddock I laughingly tell Fujiyama Crest's trainer Michael Stoute, 'If this one gets beat I'm going to blame you.' The horse's lad Derek Heeney is quick to add his own warning: 'Don't forget, Frankie, this horse is bone idle. He'll pull himself up given half a chance, so don't be afraid to give him a smack.'

We canter steadily past the stands towards the start, near the final bend, and suddenly there's this noise so loud that for a moment I think it must be a clap of thunder or a jumbo jet opening the throttles wide as it passes overhead. It's neither. It's the crowd giving me a standing ovation: people hanging over the rails shouting, cheering and applauding me. The sound and emotion goes straight through me and into my bones, rocking me to my very core. I feel as though the first race took place three and a half days rather than three and a half hours ago. It's been almost like a three-day event, the races divided into three blocks: the first three on day one, the second three on day two, and now this one all by itself. I wave back to the crowd, milking it so hard that I should be working for the Dairy Council.

I've got the worst draw of all in stall one, on the stands side, with another large field of 18 runners. It's a big ask to make my way across without encountering trouble, but the way I feel I have nothing to lose.

We set off. We immediately begin to edge, ever so quietly, across the runners nearest to us. It takes the best part of two and a half furlongs to get across to the far rail and claim the narrowest of leads, where I let Fuji stride: he's got a long stride and runs best when not worrying about other horses around him. He briefly loses his back legs as another horse clips his heels, but gets his rhythm back without disaster.

We freewheel down the hill towards Swinley Bottom, moving comfortably out on our own. I begin counting down the furlong markers. As we race over the road crossing with three furlongs left I start to hunt Fuji along, pinching an extra length or two, but all the time I'm wondering how much longer we can hold on. The crowd holler, sensing that the impossible is unfolding in front of their eyes. Into the straight, and the roar! It takes a second or two to arrive as the sound travels, and when it hits us it's like an actual pressure wave.

Fuji's tiring, running out of gas. His stride is slowing and shortening, his head dipping down to the ground: that familiar sensation every jockey knows when it gradually seems that your horse is running through treacle. I can hear Pat's whip, each whack louder and louder as he gets closer. Now I can see him out of the corner of my eye. Fuji's beyond tired, numb with exhaustion, running on empty: barely managing to put one leg in front of the other as Northern Fleet closes in remorselessly. *Keep going, keep going, for God's sake concentrate.* Fuji's almost unconscious, drawing deep on a reservoir we didn't know he possessed. He's running on fumes and so am I, because today's finally catching up with me. *Come on. Come on. Who stole the finish line?* I beg him for one last effort. He's given everything. One last push, Fiji. Dig deeper than you ever have before.

The line coming up to meet us, and Pat almost alongside …

Fuji's all out, in every way, as we cross the line. Some horses keep running for a furlong after the finish line, but within five strides he's stopped dead.

The world goes a bit strange: the sky seems suddenly darker, people moving in slow motion, and when I come back to the enclosure there's a sea of people everywhere, all going berserk. They're hanging off lamp posts, standing on railings, anywhere they can get a view. Jason Weaver rides over on Flocheck before raising my hand as if I've just won a world title fight. I certainly feel as if I've gone 15 rounds.

I lean down, hug Fuji's neck and manage one final flying dismount. It seems a long, long way down to the ground. The crowd give me three cheers. I throw my goggles among them, grab some champagne and rush round the enclosure like a Grand Prix driver, spraying the bubbly in all directions. I leap into the arms of my trusty valet Dave Currie, who's looked after me ever since I began racing professionally in this country: and what a coincidence that Dave's dad Fred looked after Alec Russell when he rode his six winners at Bogside in 1957.

If this last race had been first I'd never have dared to be so positive on Fujiyama Crest, and we almost certainly wouldn't have won. But when you're on a high you have an edge, and I've never been higher than after winning the previous six races. That's what's made the difference between victory and defeat. Pat's about the only person in the place who's not totally delighted. It's not that he's angry with me – we're good friends and I have huge respect for him – but he's such a ferocious competitor that finishing second to me for the third time in an afternoon will really stick in his craw.

It's also a reminder that this is a hard game, harder than a lot of people realise. There are those who'll suggest that the other jockeys 'gave' me the last race. That's complete rubbish. We might all be friends in the weighing room, but once we're out on the track there's no quarter asked for or given. None of them have glimpsed so much as a sniff of a winner, and I've been taking bread from their mouths all afternoon, so the idea that they'd stand aside just to watch me make history is ludicrous.

I'm dragged, pulled and shoved every which way at once as everybody wants a piece of me. 'I've never seen the like of it,' Brough Scott says. 'Never heard anything on a racetrack to equal it. It was the most exhilarating, most "to think that I was even there" moment the game will ever see.'

I find a moment to ring Catherine and tell her, and then I phone my dad in Gran Canaria.

'The Teletext's on the blink,' he says.

'Why?'

'It says you won all seven.'

'I did.'

For once he's speechless.

Still wearing my blue and pink silks, I sign several thousand racecards, newspapers, scraps of paper and backs of envelopes, including one for John Bolton, who's won £500,000 on an accumulator, and many others who say they've enjoyed the biggest wins of their lives.

The last race was at 5.35 p.m. I don't leave the course till 8. The sky's darkening by the time I get into the car. After every meeting I have a post-mortem with myself, thinking about what I could have done to improve my performance that day. But today? Today I won seven out of seven. I did everything right. It's never happened before, and it'll probably never happen again.

Andy Keats is waiting to drive me home, and he's as happy as everyone else.

Everybody but me, that is.

I'm suddenly overwhelmed with exhaustion: a crash from the high of the last few hours, everything catching up with me all at once.

'Give me a few minutes,' I say, and I compose myself before asking him to start the car.

The phone rings all the way back, and when we finally get home, Simon Crisford and Pete Burrell come round for a glass or two of bubbly. I start to feel better – at least until Catherine says that we have to go to her friend's twenty-first birthday party in Cambridge.

'You must be joking,' I say.

I'm exhausted: bone tired, absolutely fucked. All I want to do is flop at home, eat some food and try to process what's happened today.

'I'm not joking.'

'I just won seven races! And I've got another full day tomorrow. I'm shattered. I want to put my feet up.'

'It's always what you want to do, isn't it? It's always you who can't go out to dinner, who goes to bed early, who's never around for me. You never do anything for me!'

She's got a point, of course she has, and on any other night I'd happily go, but tonight I wouldn't want to go out even if it was to Buckingham Palace. Catherine insists, so I think, *All right, here we go.*

We jump in the car and drive to the party. I have one drink.

'Are you happy now?' I ask. 'We've been. I've had a drink. I want to go home.'

We argue all the way back in the car, and when we sleep that night it's back to back, each trying to hog the duvet and pull it off the other. The night of my greatest triumph and I'm not speaking to my fiancée. Nice one, Frankie.

The next morning I go downstairs to get the papers from the front doorstep: I always get them delivered on a Sunday. I'm in a T-shirt and my underpants. I open the door bleary-eyed, reach for the papers … and see three tiers of paparazzi, reporters and TV cameras! It's like being back at Marylebone police station three years ago, though at least this time they're here because I've done something good rather than bad.

I grab the papers, slam the door shut and ring Pete.

'Mate,' I say, 'it's gone ballistic.'

I'm on the front page of every paper, every single one. It's my first inkling that life will never be the same again. For me, seven out of seven is an amazing story, and I know it'll be all over the sports pages, but the front pages too? No, I never expected that. My seven has cost the bookies £40 million, enough to move the stock market as investors sell shares in bookmakers. Racing's all about gambling, and usually the bookmakers win: but this time the general public won, so it's a fairy tale. For plenty of people my seven means a holiday, a washing machine, money to feed their family. I go on breakfast TV and present a cheque for £550,000 to a punter called Darren Yates who bet big on me. Pete's phone is ringing red-hot, so much so that it actually breaks down and he hurls it into the Thames. All the big chat shows have me on – Clive Anderson, Michael Parkinson, Terry Wogan. I even present *Top of the Pops*. I make hay, and why not? We take evening appearances where we can, but not daytime ones, as I don't want to interfere with my racing schedule.

I love all this stuff. I won't pretend that I'm not doing it for myself, because of course I am, but I'm also doing it for racing, to give it a good image, a leg-up in the public consciousness. You need the riding chops to be able to pull seven races off and the personality to exploit that to the public, and I'm one of the few jockeys who has both, so I sort of think it's my responsibility.

I go to Tokyo to race the Japan Cup on Singspiel. If I'd thought Hong Kong was crazy, this is another level entirely: 150,000 people at racetracks every weekend, and all of them going mad for the gambling and the passion. Some people camp out overnight by the racecourse so they can get the best places on the rails for the big meetings. Some famous Japanese jockeys have to disguise themselves when they go out, because they're as famous as footballers are over here and they get mobbed in public. Even I get followed around the streets and constantly asked for autographs and pictures. I love it, of course: not just the attention, but the passion and the culture too, the intensity of it all.

The Japan Cup is one of the richest races in the year, up there with the Breeders' Cup, the Melbourne Cup and the Arc as one of the great end-of-year races. And together with the Japanese filly Fabulous la Fouine, we give the crowd a race to remember. Singspiel ran a fever when he first arrived in Japan, and though the vets got it down fast, you still never know in a tight race how much that illness might have taken out of a horse. We race neck and neck down the home straight and it's nip and tuck at the finish, so close that the judges need a photograph. Singspiel's no stranger to photo finishes – he's been in six and lost all but one – but this time he, and I, are on the right side of it, and we win by a nose.

Catherine and I want a summer wedding, but when we sit down to look at the racing calendar we find that our choice of dates is limited. In fact, there's only one possible day: Saturday, 20 July 1997. Every other weekend we're racing Saturdays and Sundays.

I'm due to ride Benny the Dip in the 1997 Derby for John, as Godolphin don't have a ride in the race. Benny the Dip's a good horse and well-priced at 11/1: in an open field that makes him third favourite, and I fancy my chances. Then, with only a few days left, Sheikh Mohammed thinks Bold Demand has a chance and pays the supplementary fee to enter him at the last minute. As stable jockey I have to ride Bold Demand, so Willie Ryan gets Benny the Dip and … well, you can guess the rest. Benny the Dip wins by a short head from Silver Patriarch, and I'm ninth.

These things happen all the time in racing, and it's never as simple as saying, 'Oh, if I'd ridden instead then we'd still have won.' There are so many different factors which go into determining how a race plays out: it's not remotely the case that you could swap all the jockeys around and it would play out the same way as the actual race does. But in the past three years I've finished second, third, and been forced to give up a ride on the eventual winner. It's hard to escape the simple four-word feeling: *I'll never win this.*

Things the public don't see: inside the weighing room. This is for the jockeys and valets only, our one private space in an arena where we're otherwise on show the whole time. We have such fun in here: endless banter, jokes and card games. 'Come on, lads, time to saddle up', and the cries of, 'Just finishing this game!' Some of the quietest guys in public are the most animated and funniest behind the door of the weighing room. It reminds me of my mother's tales of her days in the travelling circus. We travel together, we're with each other more than we are with our own families half the time, we know each other's strengths and weaknesses. We are a family in our own way. A family of very small men, and I guess pretty dysfunctional in some ways – aren't all families? – but a family nonetheless.

My wedding to Catherine is a beautiful day, every bit as wonderful as I'd always hoped. The highlight is when Ronnie Wood borrows a guitar from the band, fashions a plectrum from a broken bottle and sings 'Amazing Grace' with such beauty and passion that it has us all in tears.

Godolphin go from strength to strength and size to size. Four horses become 40. Forty horses become a hundred. The stallions and mares breed, and they also buy horses at the sales. The empire grows and grows, and I feel unbelievably lucky to be a part of it.

Another year, another Derby. I'm on Cape Verdi, a filly who won the 1000 Guineas by five lengths and therefore starts as favourite. But to me she's something of a false favourite. She has a lot of question marks hanging over her, and so it proves in the race. I finish ninth.

Again. That's pretty much the full house of nearlys now: third in 1995, second in 1996, jacked off the winner in 1997, and now a favourite which didn't come through in 1998.

Relations with my dad are more stop-start than rush-hour traffic. We're OK for a while, and then something triggers it and we don't speak for another few months or years. I try to help broker some sort of rapprochement between him and Sandra, my sister, but it's so hard. They're two of the most stubborn people in the world, and neither of them wants to give in. They replay the same old arguments again and again, him saying she shouldn't have run away from home and her saying she does what the hell she wants and he never understands why she did it. I try and try, and sometimes they agree to meet up, but it always falls through, with one or the other thinking better of it or not turning up.

And of course this in turn causes problems between my old man and me, because I tell him I hate to see my sister not treated the same way as I am. There's no winner here, I tell him. It's all pointless because one day we're all going to die sad. Why the stand-off? Just to prove a point, that's what it is. Just to prove a point. We have a big argument and just stop speaking. Each time it happens it's strange to readjust – he's the one I talk to about my races, he's the one I can't bullshit – but like anything, I get used to it. His presence fades, like a photograph left out in the sun: but it never vanishes, not completely.

Even though I'm pretty much at the top of my game, I still get the odd reminder not to be complacent or to take things for granted. In this sport you're only as good as your next race, never mind your last one.

I'm riding Swain in the 1998 Breeders' Cup Classic, and I screw it up. Silver Charm, one of the favourites, is a real fighter, at his best when there's another horse alongside. And he has history with Swain, beating him by a short head in the Dubai World Cup earlier this year. I therefore decide to challenge Silver Charm wide, stay away from him and try to steal a march that way. But when, in the closing stages, I can't get past him I panic and go way over the top. I hit Swain far too many times on his left side and he veers right as we pass beneath the floodlights. The drift costs me momentum, and that lost momentum costs me the race.

It's total amateur hour: I haven't done anything like this for years. Why did I mess it up? Lots of reasons. I was under pressure, it was cold, I was nervous, expectations of me were high, and I was out of my comfort zone racing far from home. But I've raced, and won, plenty of times in those conditions.

I'm so embarrassed that I lie to Saeed bin Suroor about what happened.

'Swain got spooked by the floodlights,' I say.

Saeed knows I'm covering up for my mistake. He's way too canny and smart to be taken in.

'I can't see that the grandstand lights were to blame,' he tells the press. 'All the people watching the race there and on the TV and all over the world know he made a mistake. That's what happens in a race. It's a shame. Frankie is a big name and he's our jockey. At the same time, I'd like to see him ride better than this. I know he is a brilliant jockey. He's one of the best jockeys in Europe. It's normal to make a mistake.'

It's a vote of confidence I badly need and really appreciate. I'm a lot harder on myself than they are on me, and my anguish is exacerbated by the reaction of the American press. Bill Finley writes that 'Swain would probably have won if anybody but Frankie Dettori was on his back', and Vic Ziegel adds that 'Dettori's excuse was a lot more creative than his ride'.

Despite Godolphin's support – Sheikh Mohammed himself rings me the next day to say, 'Don't stress' – it gnaws at me for a long time afterwards. It's only one reversal, but it assumes such importance. Partly this is a good thing, because it shows how high my standards are these days, but people in the stables are still taking the mick about it months later, well into the new 1999 season. Eventually I go to see Simon and get his reassurance that my job's not at risk.

'We'll have another chance at the Breeders' Cup this autumn,' he says. 'Store it all up.'

Catherine laughs at my habits. I can't sleep unless we have dark curtains, practically blackout strength. Then I put eye patches on, lie on my back in the coffin position and put one hand over my privates. But during the day, I always like to have the TVs on: the one in the kitchen, the big one in the sitting area, the one in my gym. I don't even have to be watching any of them. It runs in the family. Dad and Christine do the same. In their home in Sardinia there's an Italian station on for him and a French station for her. He'll be outside mowing the lawn, she'll be looking after her chickens, and those tellies are still going full blast.

This is the year I think I might break my Derby duck. I'm on Dubai Millennium, possibly the most powerful horse I've ever ridden. His name was originally Yassa, but Godolphin have changed it to Dubai Millennium because they know what a superstar he is. At full speed he seems to have the raw power of a jet plane, practically pulling my arms from my sockets when he accelerates. I'm almost afraid of that much power, as when it comes on full bore I know that I'm more or less a passenger and he's invincible. He's won easily at Doncaster and Goodwood, and when he's made favourite for the Derby it's the second year in a row that I'm riding the most-fancied mount. This time I feel the odds are fairer, though to a degree they're also reflective of the openness of the race.

Either way, it doesn't happen. Again. We're caught in traffic before the meeting, and the noise and the crowds totally spook him. It's sticky and humid, the kind of weather that sets humans and animals alike on edge, and he's sweating up and pulling in the parade ring. The moment I see him I have that sinking feeling which every jockey knows: today is not my day. Sometimes in a small meeting I can calm the horse down on the way up to the start, but not at the Derby, not with 100,000 people cheering our every move. Henry Cecil takes a fine for Kieren Fallon breaking away from the parade early, clearly fearing that Oath might act up like Dubai Millennium is. Maybe I should follow suit, but I don't think it'll make much difference. I canter up to the start, knowing that this is a total waste of time. All the energy we need for the race has gone, flown away like pollen on the Epsom breeze. He pulls like hell from the start and is struggling by the time we reach the straight. Oath wins. I finish ninth for the third year in a row. It's a record of sorts, I guess.

Leo's born just before the Arc, and that's no coincidence: we have him induced deliberately so I can go and ride knowing that he's safe and sound. Though we don't yet know it, all our children will be induced according to the dictates of the racing calendar: Ella will be a Dubai World Cup baby, Mia a Royal Ascot one, Tallula a Breeders' Cup baby, and Rocco born at the beginning of the season.

I hate the whole process. Anyone who says it's brilliant must be lying or mad. I'm sitting there helpless, sweating and worrying. I get drunk on champagne afterwards, crawl into bed with Catherine and Leo, and pass out. Catherine's less thrilled than I am at this.

When the 1999 Breeders' Cup comes round I'm ready, and I've nursed my grudge all season. This time it's held in Florida and I'm on Daylami, fresh from winning the King George and the Irish Champion Stakes. I'm more focused than I can ever remember being. I stay at the back on the inside in the opening stages as the leaders go through at a fast pace, and then gradually ease my way through to be poised fourth as we come round the final turn, with the defending champion Buck's Boy leading. I take the wide line, which may mean we run a bit further but also means we'll get a clear run. When I ask Daylami for full gas he responds emphatically. In no time at all we're clear of the field and going away with every stride. Over the last hundred metres I have tears in my eyes, and as we cross the line I'm screaming my triumph at the heavens. 'How about that, you bastards? Still think I'm a second-rate jockey?'

They say revenge is a dish best served cold. Mine is freezing.

No race I ride on Dubai Millennium can quite make up for the disappointment of the Derby, but the 2000 Dubai World Cup comes close. Not staying the distance in the Derby apart, he's won every other race he's run, so he's such a hot favourite it's almost prohibitive – and when you're riding the local hero to boot that's even more pressure. With Catherine and Leo there – it's the first big race my son's seen me ride, not that he knows too much about it – we lead almost from the start, stringing the others out like a tail behind a comet. I've never had an experience like it. He's absolutely awesome, so powerful it's truly scary. It feels like I'm sitting astride a jet engine. I feel he never even gets out of low gear:

he's cruising all the way, yet he pulls clear of some very good horses. We win by six lengths easing down. He's probably the best horse I've ever ridden, and I doubt I'll ever ride another as good.

It's quite a strange feeling, given that I'm not yet 30 and I still have a decade or more of my career left. Well, hopefully. That's what people say, isn't it? 'Hopefully', when looking into the future, just so as not to put a hex on things, because life can change and go wrong in an instant.

I'm about to find out just how true that is.

4

NEWMARKET

Thursday, 1 June 2000. It's a horrible day, windy and grey: the kind of day which doesn't have a good feel to it, the kind of day when anyone sensible would simply huddle under a duvet at home and watch an old movie on TV.

I'm flying to Goodwood, and I don't want to be the only passenger on the plane: I want some company. I ask Richard Hills and John Ferguson, but neither of them can make it. So I ring Ray Cochrane and say, 'Would you like a lift to Goodwood?' The forecast is for rain and he doesn't fancy getting drenched on his motorbike, so he jumps at the chance.

The usual plane's being serviced, so we've got a rented Piper Seneca.

'When are we getting our normal one back?' I ask Patrick Mackey, the pilot.

'As soon as possible, I hope,' he says. 'I don't like this one.'

That's not what I want to hear. Patrick's an experienced pilot and a level-headed guy. If he doesn't like it there must be a reason. But not enough of a reason not to fly, and in any case we have to get to Goodwood. The plane might not be great, but at least it works.

We get in. Patrick takes the front left-hand seat, with me directly behind him and Ray next to me. Ray and I are both facing forwards. There are rear-facing seats opposite us, but they're empty.

'Look,' says Patrick as he does the pre-flight checks, 'it's windy and it's going to be hairy, so buckle up.'

He's not wrong. We're bumping and bouncing as we accelerate down the runway, with the wind buffeting us from left to right. The left wing lifts a bit, tipping the plane to the right, and I hear a brief bang before we keep going.

Ray and I look at each other. This isn't right.

We seem to bunny hop on take-off: we get a few feet in the air, touch down, get going again.

This definitely isn't right.

We're low over the railings of the July Course, a hundred feet or so up. There's smoke coming out of the right engine, I can see the first flickering of flames, and the propeller looks as though it's damaged. That bang we heard earlier must have been it hitting the ground as the plane lurched to the side.

We tilt suddenly, hard over to the right at a crazy angle, the ground seeming almost off to my side rather than directly beneath. I brace myself in my seat, clinging onto the armrests. Patrick's fighting at the controls to keep us airborne, but it's mission impossible. We're being pulled down to the ground.

We're going to die.

We're going to die.

We're going to die.

It's so stupid. I'm in perfect health, I'm one of the best in the world at what I do, I've just won the Gold Cup, and most of all I've got a wife and baby boy I love. All about to be wiped out so close to home I can practically see my front door.

I don't even have the strength to scream or cry. What I feel most, even beyond fear, is disappointment. My life isn't flashing in front of my eyes like lots of people say it does at times like these. I'm just thinking, *Why? Why now? Why take me now?*

Finished, lights off, gone, dead: a button pressed, a life ended. It's going to hurt like hell. I hope it's quick.

We're on our side, the left wing almost vertically above the right as we dive towards the bank. The ground rushes up to meet us. There's a raised mound called the Devil's Dyke which runs between the two racecourses at Newmarket. If we crash nose first into that we'll all be killed instantly, smashed to pieces like flies on a car windscreen.

Patrick hauls at the controls for all he's worth. For a moment I think he'll pull off a miracle and clear the dyke, but then the very tip of the right wing clips the top of the bank, and that softens the impact: not enough to stop the crash, but enough to take some of the worst out of it.

We go cartwheeling into the ground on the other side of the ditch. The impact is thunder and lightning all in one, a ghastly nightmare sound of metal scraping and voices screaming which seems to go on for ever. We're totally helpless, with no control over our fate whatsoever. If we end up upside down we'll be trapped in the wreckage and burned to death when the fuel ignites. It's all down to God, physics, kismet, blind chance, call it what you want.

We smash into the ground, bounce a bit and come to rest – the right way up, mercifully. For a few seconds the world goes black, a brief moment of unconsciousness, and then I come round. My leg's in agony, and I feel something warm and sticky on my face. Blood.

I can't move. I just can't move. I'm in a sort of netherworld, half-conscious and half-alive. Things move in slow motion: a weird, disembodied feeling. Am I on the other side? Is this the afterlife?

I have 180-degree vision: I can see everything in a much wider arc, but I can't focus on anything. I see that Ray and I are still strapped in our seats. The passenger door on my left is crushed like a packet of grapes, squashed in pretty much on top of me, half-pinning me down and making sure there's no escape that way.

Patrick's slumped motionless with his head against the dashboard: certainly unconscious, maybe dead, while flames billow from the engines. Ray gives me a belt, and his voice is loud in the sudden silence. 'Get out! Frankie, get out! The plane's full of fuel.'

Then suddenly, almost with a jerk, everything speeds up, back to normal, like a record suddenly switched from 33 to 45 rpm.

The tiny door used to stow baggage immediately behind my seat is ajar. Ray kicks it open, leans forward to undo my seatbelt, drags me backwards and pushes me out of the narrow opening. It's only a foot or two down to the ground, but I land on my injured ankle and the pain is so sharp that I can do nothing but scream and lie there. Ray disappears back inside to try to get Patrick.

The left wing and engine are still intact, but the right wing's been torn pretty much clean off, the right engine is several metres away, and both propellers are smashed and ripped. The sweet smell of kerosene, overpowering and dangerous. I'm right next to a machine that's on fire and going to explode at any moment, and I can't move.

'Ray! Ray!' I'm screaming for all I'm worth, but my voice still sounds faint and distant. 'Help me!' My leg is agony, jagged shards of pain forking like lightning through me every time I move. There's so much blood that I can't see out of one eye. I wonder whether I've lost that eye. Maybe I'll be half-blind for ever.

For a moment I think Ray hasn't heard me, but then his face appears at the broken hatch. He pushes himself through, grabs my arms, drags me 20 or 30 metres away, and heads back towards the wreckage.

I can see flames beginning to appear underneath the plane. Ray doesn't care. He's insanely brave, unbelievably so. Most other people would back off now, but he has total disregard for his own safety. He forces open the pilot's door on the right-hand side, leans in, reaches towards Patrick … and a ball of fire the size of a tree spirals up, knocking Ray back with the force of the explosion. Even from where I am, I wince at the force of the blast and the rush of heat on my face. Ray staggers, recoils and struggles round to the other side of the plane to have another go through the baggage hatch.

'Get away from it!' A racecourse worker has appeared and is screaming at Ray. 'Get out of it!'

Ray either doesn't hear or doesn't care. He rips off his jacket and beats at the flames raging high and angry all around him, but to no avail. The cockpit's on fire and there's no way that anyone short of a fully equipped fire brigade is getting in there. Patrick's gone. Ray realises this and goes ballistic, hammering on the side of the plane and screaming at the heavens before collapsing in hot tears of rage and frustration. He crawls over and hugs me, and that's how we stay for a while, huddled together in shock like two small woodland animals.

The army turn up. I don't know if they were nearby or what, but anyway, they're here quickly: a plane going down near a racecourse with flames and smoke everywhere is hard to miss, I guess. Then the paramedics arrive, and a lot more people from the racecourse. The paramedics strap an oxygen mask on me. I see Peter Amos, who's in charge of the Jockey Club Estates. He sparks up a cigarette. 'Captain,' I say as best I can through the mask, 'what I'm breathing is a lot better for me than what you're breathing is for you.'

The soldiers load me into a helicopter. The last thing I want is to be airborne again – the hospital's only 10 miles away so an ambulance will be fine if it's all the same, thanks guys. But they're having none of it. So I'm taken on a helicopter to Addenbrooke's, all trussed up on a stretcher.

We're put in a remote ward, just Ray and me. We're pumped full of painkillers and morphine, so everything becomes a bit surreal again. They operate on my leg and take some skin to do plastic surgery on my face. Ray's got third-degree burns on his hands and elsewhere, and he's all smashed up from the crash.

'You don't look too good, Ray,' I say.

He looks at me and laughs.

'You don't look that flash yourself, mate. I've got to be honest.'

Reporters are sneaking in dressed as doctors and nurses, and only hospital security stop them finding the room where Ray and I are recuperating.

The door opens. I think it'll be one of the people who've been in and out of here since the crash: Catherine, Pete, Sheikh Mohammed, maybe one of the jockeys.

It's none of them.

It's my dad.

I don't really remember much of what we say, because that whole period is a bit of a haze. But I do remember being so glad that he's here, and laughing that it's taken a near-death experience to bring us back together after two or three years of not speaking. We feel the same thing: what's the point of all this arguing when I was dead two minutes ago? But God, it takes a plane crash to force us to make up.

No matter how much we might argue and fight, he's still my dad, I'm still his son, and we love each other. All the other crap goes out of the window at a time like this. It's not about who's right or wrong. It's just a father and a son and the love between them, and even at our worst times I've never doubted his love for me: just the way he's chosen to show it.

After a week they put me in a wheelchair and discharge me. It's surprisingly hard to adjust to what once seemed such a normal life. It feels like a year since the crash rather than a week, and in all that time I've been in a cocoon: everything done for me, every meal brought, everyone coming to see me. Now even everyday sights and sounds seem a little overwhelming.

Patrick's funeral is in St Joseph's Catholic Church at Newbury. The press are there but I ignore them, and I try to blot out the fact that people are looking at me and Ray while pretending not to. Even with the ones I know who are full of genuine concern, I feel – well, not shame as such, but certainly some discomfort. How are you, Frankie? Well, I'm here, for a start, and that alone makes me luckier than Patrick. I can't shake the feeling I've had pretty much since the crash, and certainly since the morphine and painkillers wore off: why did he die when I didn't? He was such a good guy, and 52 is no age to die. When I talk to his family my words sound so inadequate, but maybe any and all words would sound inadequate.

I watch the Derby a few days later. This is the race I've set my heart on winning above every other, the one which each year breaks my heart all over again: but for once I don't care. I watch it through a fog of indifference. There are four Godolphin runners in it, but none of them place. Best of the Bests, which I'd probably have been riding, finishes fourth. That makes it slightly easier to bear. Of course I'd like a Godolphin horse to win, but after setting my heart so much on winning this race above all others I don't think I could bear it if someone else won on a horse which should have been mine.

I remember the promise I made to myself as a little boy to own a Ferrari before I turned 30. I'm 29 now, and the crash has shown me that life's all about seizing the day.

What the hell am I waiting for? I think. *I'm getting that damn Ferrari now.*

I go to the dealership and buy a 360 Modena.

I can't sit around too much: it drives me mad. I get into my morning suit, Catherine drops me at Dalham Hall Stud, and I get a lift in a helicopter to watch Dubai Millennium run in the Prince of Wales at Ascot. I wonder whether the helicopter will trigger flashbacks in me, but it doesn't: the whole interior layout of the craft and angle of take-off are different, and that's the important thing.

Walking through the parade ring, I hear people cheering and clapping. *Oh, the Queen's here*, I think, and look round to see where she is. She's nowhere in sight, and gradually I realise that the applause is for me. I'm very touched, and I try to show it without breaking down totally. Racing fans are the best, they really are.

It's Dubai Millennium's tenth race, but the first one I haven't ridden. Jerry Bailey does the honours in my absence, and they win by eight lengths. Last year's Derby apart, Dubai Millennium has a perfect record. What a horse! I can't wait to get back on him again. He's my light at the end of the tunnel. Every time I get on a treadmill and it's agony, I think of Dubai Millennium, grit my teeth and keep going.

* * *

The phone rings. It's Simon.

'Frankie, there's no easy way to say this, so I'll just do it straight. Dubai Millennium's broken his leg.'

I almost laugh, it's so ridiculous. It never rains, but it pours. My leg's broken, my horse's leg is broken. It nearly does me in completely.

No, I vow. I'll heal, Dubai Millennium will heal, and we'll ride again.

I'll fly in jumbo jets and I'll fly in helicopters, but light aircraft? Not a chance.

I develop claustrophobia too. I used to laugh at my mum when I was a kid and she'd have to have the window open, or when she wouldn't go in a lift, but now it's happening to me.

I try to be less stressed and more laid-back: not as aggressive, not as competitive. I change my attitude. From now on I'm not going to go round chasing endless winners.

I'm back riding at Newmarket two months later. I notch a couple of winners, Atlantis Prince and Dim Sums. I don't know exactly what number of career winners they give me, but they're numbers one and two of my new career and life.

Riding's my job, so I've come back as soon as I'm

ready. But there's a difference between being physically ready and mentally ready. I'm the first, but I'm not the second. It's not something the casual viewer would notice, but it's clear to me: all the things I take for granted are just slightly off. It's very hard to explain, but I'm just not ready.

I keep going nonetheless. I have to. We all have to.

Ray's also back riding, but his burns and neck injury are agony, and he's not – he can't be – the same rider he was before. He's suffering physically and mentally. His neck injury means that he's perhaps one fall away from being paralysed, and that's no way to live your life or run your career.

'Ray,' I say, 'why don't you pack it in and be my agent? Hang up your boots and your breeches and come and work with me. No one knows the racing game like you. We'd be a great team.'

So that's what he does, and that's what we are. It's also the only way I can even begin to pay him back for saving my life. Because he *did* save my life, simple as that. If he hadn't first kicked me out of the plane and then dragged me away, I'd have been caught up in the fireball and burnt to death. It's one of several lucky escapes that day. If Richard had been on board, he'd have been sitting opposite me, facing backwards, and instead of smashing into an empty seat on impact I'd have smashed into him and been killed as certainly as if I'd smashed into a stone pillar.

It's not just races which can hinge on small margins. It's lives too.

Fujiyama Crest's entered in the 2000 Malvern bloodstock sales. He reminds me of Gérard Depardieu: big, gangly, no great beauty but full of personality. To me, of course, he will always be priceless. He was the last (and least likely) of my seven winners at Ascot, and without him my career and life would be half of what they are.

I can't let him go up for auction. I have to buy him first. I get in touch with the sellers and we hammer out a deal. They know why I want him and how badly, so they can play hardball on the price a bit, but we all also know that there are no guarantees at bloodstock sales, so a keen buyer is never to be sniffed at.

We agree a price and Fuji comes to live with us. Over the years he'll become a much-loved part of the family, endlessly patient with my kids and all their friends who ride him. Every time I go out to the paddock to feed him, I'm glad I've been able to pay him back for giving me not just the race of his life, but the race of mine too.

* * *

Everybody just expects me to carry on as normal, to ride as normal, to be Frankie as normal. 'Oh, it's Frankie, he'll be all right.' No one wants to be normal more than I do, but only now do I really appreciate something fundamental about my life: that nothing in it has ever been normal. It's not normal to have a dad who's champion jockey, who sent me away to a different country aged 14 and whom I sometimes don't talk to for years on end. It's not normal to have scores of reporters at a police station when you go there. It's not normal to ride seven winners in seven races at Ascot. It's not normal to survive a plane crash which nine times out of 10 would have killed you. And it's not normal to have done all this before the age of 30.

Maybe I take that abnormality so much for granted that it's become normal, and deep down I am still the same old Frankie. At least that's what I tell myself. But it's not true. Other people notice it, even if I don't. You're a bit quiet, Frankie. You're not your usual self. Nothing huge or of too much concern: just a little off my baseline levels.

I don't see a counsellor. I'm Italian. By the time I've told the story to a million family and friends, what else is there to say? I think I'm OK, but inside the same questions are churning around over and over again. Why me? Why not me? Why did I survive when Patrick didn't? The fear of knowing that death could be so close and unexpected, and that next time I might not be so lucky. These thoughts tumble over each other like clothes in a washing machine.

I'm looking for an answer, and it takes me a while to realise there is no answer. Things happen, and the more I look for a reason, the more confused and disappointed I get. I realise that the only thing I can control is my reaction to what's happened, so that's the only thing which is important.

I can't pinpoint a time when it suddenly gets better. Maybe that's not the way it works. Maybe I just recover so slowly that it's almost imperceptible. I've got a good family and good friends, and together with the passing of time they help me climb out of it. It's still there at the back of my mind the whole time, but gradually it feels less raw. If I have to talk about it then it still upsets me, but other than that I manage to keep it walled off pretty well. Nothing good comes from dwelling on it obsessively.

Ray and I never talk about it. Not once. It probably scarred him more than me because he saw the whole thing, he was the one who tried to rescue Patrick. I was lying on the ground, half out of it. He pretty much saw Patrick die in front of him. He couldn't have done more. Patrick was three feet away from him, but there was nothing he could have done to help. Three feet away

– you can reach out and touch three feet away. It would haunt anybody. So he handles it his way and I handle it mine. It's something that's personal between me and him. In any case, what's there to talk about? You saved my life, mate. Thanks. He knows how grateful I am and always will be for that. It's something we share at such a deep level that we don't need to talk about it. It's just there.

Dubai Millennium has grass sickness, which paralyses his intestines. Godolphin have the best vets in the business, and they do everything they can to save him. It's not enough. He has to be put down.

It's always a wrench when this happens. The accountants will wince at the bottom line – imagine all the stud fees he's missed out on, as he is only five – but for me it's much more personal. When the best horse I've ever ridden dies so quickly and so long before his time, a little piece of my heart goes with him, and the only crumb of comfort is knowing how lucky I was to have ridden him and felt the afterburners ignite beneath me when he kicked for home.

One of the great things about this sport is that I'm always learning. It doesn't matter how many races I've ridden or winners I've had, I still don't know everything, and I never will.

The 2001 Irish Champion Stakes at Leopardstown are a good example of this. I'm on Fantastic Light, and our main rival is Galileo. We sit down to discuss what tactics to use.

'I want to stalk Galileo all the way and kick in the last furlong,' I say.

'Fantastic Light should keep up at the front,' Sheikh Mohammed says.

'He idles up front,' I reply. 'He's better coming from behind.'

'No. Don't let Galileo get ahead of you, whatever happens.'

That's the end of the discussion. It's Sheikh Mohammed's horse, so whatever he says goes.

Richard Hills paces us on Give the Slip. With two furlongs left, he leaves enough room for me to come through on the outside and get the jump on Galileo. We're neck and neck all the way to the line, but Fantastic Light wants it just that little bit more and prevails at the last. If we'd run it my way, would we have won? Who knows? But we ran it Sheikh Mohammed's way and we won, therefore he was right.

I finish 2001 with 94 wins. Leaving aside last year, when I only rode 47 having missed so much of the season recovering from the crash, it's the first time since 1991 that I haven't reached a century. Part of it is by choice: I've decided to ride fewer races and not chase every single opportunity. But still.

I'm asked to be a team captain on the BBC's *A Question of Sport*. It's such an institution that of course I say yes: it's an honour to be following in the footsteps of all the famous sportsmen who've come before, not least my old chum Willie Carson.

The first thing I discover is that it's a lot harder than it looks. For a start, I'm filling big shoes by replacing John Parrott, who's been such an established and integral part of the programme, and that puts pressure on me to step up to the mark. Then there's the Italian factor: a lot of my sporting references are Italian rather than English, and when the banter comes thick and fast, sometimes I find myself mentally translating into Italian and back again, and by the time I've got my head round that we're three jokes further down the line. Finally, the schedule's punishing. We do three shows back to back, so I have to bring three sets of clothes with me, and each show takes about an hour and a half to film (even though the finished product is only half an hour). I'm so tired out by it that I find myself napping between shows.

On one show there's a round of anagrams which, when rearranged, will give the name of a famous sportsman or woman. The one they give me is TRINKET RIDE OAF. I'm not good at these things at the best of times, let alone in a studio with lights and an audience. My mind goes blank. It could be anyone. The audience are very amused at my agonising, until eventually I spread my hands wide. 'I give up, Sue.'

Sue Barker can hardly contain her laughter as she tells me that the answer is … Frankie Dettori!

Some trainers are upset when they see me on the show: they think I'm spending too much time in TV studios and not enough time training. Of course, those programmes are filmed months in advance, and I deliberately do them out of season when I have the minimum amount of other commitments. But when I end the 2002 season with only 69 wins, I start to think that maybe those trainers have a point.

I like to have Catherine and the children with me in Dubai if possible during the winter training out there, but sometimes it's not – nursery commitments and so on – and then it gets lonely. Everyone thinks sun, sea and sand is paradise, and in lots of ways it is, especially at a time when back home it's snow or mud, but it's a lot less fun when there's no one around to share it with.

I'm a people person: I like them around and I like to be around them.

The helicopter to Ascot's about to take off when I get a sudden panic attack. I know the symptoms by now: shortness of breath, tight chest, face slick with sweat, and most of all a voice inside my head barking, *Get out! Get out!* It's all I can do not to open the door. But if I give in then I know the next attack will be worse. In life you're told to always get back on the horse: well, for someone who spends his life on a horse then maybe this is the next one along. Stay in the helicopter. I open the *Racing Post* and study the form as hard as I can, thinking about the races ahead and the tactics I need: anything and everything to keep me from focusing on the here and now.

It'll be here all my life, I realise, and I don't know when it's going to affect me. Sometimes it feels like it happened 30 years ago: sometimes it feels like just now. The subconscious can be so powerful, and few people who haven't been through that kind of trauma really understand it. I get to cope with it and learn to live with it, but I can't explain what I lived through and how it will stay with me for the rest of my life.

*   *   *

The French rugby player Thomas Castaignède is on *A Question of Sport*. We're between takes, just chatting.

'How long have you been retired?' he asks.

It stops me in my tracks. He's not saying it as a joke or to be a jerk or anything – he's a lovely guy. He's asking the question because that's what he genuinely believes, and who can blame him? That's the assumption he's made: I'm here giving lots of time to a TV programme, I'm doing lots of other stuff in the public eye, so how could I possibly still be a jockey? How could I have the time or the focus for that?

I think about the question for days afterwards: it's like picking at a scab. I've got a lot more to offer my life and the racing public. I don't want to be recognised just from television. I'm a jockey and I'm damn good at it.

It hurts me deep inside. I want to be recognised because I'm one of the greats, not because I'm doing quiz shows on TV. I'm trying to get the balance right between the racing world and the celebrity world, but maybe it's a circle that can't be squared. Doing both means I'm not doing either that well.

It's funny, the things which make a difference: Thomas's chance remark will end up changing so much.

*　*　*

The 2003 season starts well. I win the Dubai World Cup on Moon Ballad. The richest day's racing in the world, £500,000 in two hours, thank you very much. But it's the worst thing that could happen to me because I take my foot off the pedal, sit back a little bit and expect everything's going to come easy.

It doesn't. Once the others get a foot in the door then they take over. I get shafted a few times on the racecourse, and I don't seem invincible any more. No one's going to give this to me. I have to earn my way back, and I can't. It's a crap summer. A crap, crap, crap summer. Everything I touch turns to shit. I'd get beaten in a walkover. A bad year happens to everyone, no matter how good they are. It happens to Ferrari, it happens to Manchester United, it happens to Godolphin and Coolmore. When things aren't going so well, it's like a marriage. You have to be frank, and I am. So there are times with everyone I work with when we argue like cats and dogs, but that's the way I prefer it. We say our piece, get it out in the open and move on.

But it makes little difference. I feel that David Loder is increasingly preferring Jamie Spencer to me on some horses, which leads to us arguing. I try hard to rectify the situation, but of course that just makes things worse: I'm tense, I'm forcing things. Gaps which used to appear never do. My timing's all wrong. It's like strikers in football: when they're out of form they can't score even if they walk the ball in. The same is happening to me.

I'm not doing what every good jockey should do, which is to relax and tune myself not only into the horse's mood but also into the ebb and flow of the races. Animals have a sixth sense. The horses feel my low mood and they don't perform to their best. I do everything I can to change things – take a step back, take a step forward, watch the videos again and again, read the form more, but it's still not coming naturally. The harder I try the worse I ride, so I try even harder and ride even worse, and on it goes in a vicious circle. In trying to get out of the hole, I just make a bigger hole. I become depressed, lethargic, moody. I'm a complete nuisance: moping around, succeeding only in depressing myself, no use to anybody.

To add insult to injury, many people think my problem is not that I'm trying too hard but that I'm trying too little. 'Frankie doesn't care any more,' they're saying. 'He's too rich, too complacent, too in love with being famous.' They don't say it to my face, of course, but I hear it on the grapevine anyway. They look at the showmanship and the TV appearances and mistake them for my not caring. Everybody jumps on the bandwagon, gets the knives out and kicks me in the arse.

I go to Sardinia with my dad and we have a good old heart to heart. For all the strife between us sometimes, he's the one guy I really need to talk to at times like this.

'You need to ride more.'

'More? Not less?'

'That's right. More. But there's a catch. You need to go to all the small meetings, the ones you've been missing out as you ride the big races more and more. Do this and two things will happen. One, you'll get more winners, which will help restore your confidence. Two, you'll remind yourself of the hunger you need, and indeed of the hunger you started out with. Either way, don't overthink it. Just get out there and ride. Just go back to basics again. Racing's a simple sport at heart, like most sports.'

That's just what I do. I go to Baden-Baden on a 10/1 chance, and I win. I don't stress, I don't force things: I trust in my instincts and it works. It's the start of a turnaround. In September alone I ride 30 winners, which, given that I was on 50 for the entire season before, shows how much good the change has done. By the time the season's done, I've just about sneaked over the century mark, and end with 101.

* * *

We have a code in the weighing room. When you come in as an apprentice, your peg is the one at the far end of the room. The most senior guys are next to the door, because after the door you're out. When I started the room was full of men like Walter, Ray, Greville Starkey and Pat: now, at the end of the 2003 season, Pat follows the other three into retirement. He hands the baton to Richard Hills, but Richard doesn't want to sit by the door, even though it's his privilege to do so. So I get to be the one by the door, the prime seat in the weighing room. It means I'm senior, accomplished, I've done it. But it means all those things only because I started at the other end of the room and worked my way through, just like everybody else. And these guys I ride against: I need them all. They're my medicine for getting up in the morning.

After the desolate summer, a long winter. I look inside myself. Was that late summer and autumn flourish a one-off, or was it the harbinger of something new, something better? I remember the character who a decade ago kissed his girlfriend goodbye and went to Morocco for Christmas: not to party and have fun, but to prepare himself like a Spartan for an assault on the championship. Where's that character gone now? He's still there somewhere deep inside, but he's hard to find beyond the hollow of easy celebrity and the persona the public know.

There's Frankie the TV personality, the cheeky Italian charmer, and there's Lanfranco the jockey. Both are parts of me and both are equally genuine, but only one is the core of my being. Ever since the crash I've been telling myself that there's more to life than being a jockey. I've wanted to be this family man who does some nice safe work on the telly. But I need to get back to being me, and that means starting from scratch.

Catherine sits me down.

'Well, it's your choice. You can let the crash dictate your life and spend the next 20 or 30 years being a full-time celebrity.' I remember what I thought of those guys in the Met Bar when I was just starting out as a pro and wanting to be part of the scene: what's the point of celebrity, and what do these people actually do? 'Or you can get back to being what you're fucking good at, which is riding horses. You choose. But I know one thing for sure: you can't be a full-time jockey part-time.'

She's so strong, and she's so right. I've never shied away from putting myself out front, whether it's the flying dismount, presenting *Top of the Pops* or doing *A Question of Sport*. I go in the local paper shop here and the guy says, 'It's about time you won seven out of seven in Dubai.' And I say, 'Yeah, tell you what, I'll do it on

Dubai World Cup day.' But it all depends on *where* I put myself out front, and at the end of the day that has to be the place where I'm happiest: going 40 mph on the back of a horse.

I enjoy television, but it lacks that buzz of winning a race, that special feeling of being the best. *A Question of Sport* is neither here nor there, really, is it? I've become a part-timer. The only way to be a great jockey is to be out there every day, giving it loads. So I give up *A Question of Sport*. I've given it a good go but enough is enough. I don't just walk out on the BBC, of course. I've got a contract, we've got shows booked in, and I'm going to honour that. But Pete talks to them and says, 'Listen, when it comes to renewing I'm afraid we're not going to, and it's not because Frankie's not enjoying it or we want more money or anything. It's just that he wants to get back to being a jockey.'

There are those who say, 'Well, if you're that serious then you should ditch the restaurants too', because by now Marco Pierre White and I have started this chain called Frankie's. But the truth is that those restaurants take up almost none of my time at all. It's my name above the door, literally, but I'm very much a sleeping partner. Marco does it all. I mean, why wouldn't he? He doesn't cadge a ride in the 1000 Guineas, and I don't stand in a restaurant kitchen barking orders at everyone.

If I'm going to be all in, it has to mean absolutely everything. I'm going to try for champion jockey again in 2004.

It's exactly what I said I wouldn't do after the plane crash, that I wouldn't just chase winners wherever they come: but things change and this is what I need. Kieren has won seven of the last eight titles, so he's the man I need to go after. I won't fly in small planes to distant meetings, so that's going to make it hard for me, but I'll still give it a go. I think 150 winners will be a good result: any more than that is a bonus.

I ride five winners at Folkestone early in April, and that shows me that I'm back on form with a vengeance. When you're hot you're hot, and that transmits itself not just to the horses I ride, but to my rivals too. *You thought I was complacent*, I think. *You thought I didn't fancy it. But like Arnie, I'm back.* I'm riding in small meetings again, those ones on cold and horrible Monday afternoons that I haven't ridden for years. It's really hard work, but I love it. I feel good, my wife feels good, my kids feel good and my friends feel good, because the real me is back and doing well. I've got back everything that had gone missing from my life.

*　　*　　*

Markers come and go.

Seventh in the Derby on Snow Light. Who wins? Kieren, of course. It makes me even more determined to beat him to champion jockey.

My two-thousandth win, on Doyen in the King George. The Queen hands me the trophy.

'That's my fourth King George,' I say.

She looks at me and raises an eyebrow. 'Lester won seven.'

That's me told.

The media and public love the contest, not least because Kieren and I are such different characters. I'm the extrovert, garrulous and a showman: he's the introvert, a brooding silent assassin. I'm the son of a champion jockey: Kieren's from a tough background and fought his way up on the hard northern circuit. As racing correspondent Greg Wood says, 'Horses seem to run for Dettori because they want to. They seem to run for Fallon because they would rather not find out what will happen if they don't.'

This idea of me as the good boy and him as the bad guy is hard to shake. But I just want to keep racing him so I can beat him fair and square over a whole season. And deep down, where it matters, we're very much the same: we both want desperately to win.

I see more of Kieren than I do of Catherine. I like him. We're out there eight hours a day scrapping it out, day in, day out. Along with Mick Kinane, he's the best jockey I've ridden against – I never rode against Lester at his peak – and Kieren's definitely the hardest to beat. When I follow him, I never know which way he's going to go or what card he's going to play.

He's an obsessive guy who just won't be stopped once he gets something in his head. He takes up golf, and rather than just play a round or two for fun he tackles it like a madman. He plays before racing, after racing and even between racing. That's Kieren. He wants to win at everything. He says nothing. He just goes out there and does it.

It's the first day of September. I turn on the breakfast news.

'Champion jockey Kieren Fallon was arrested at dawn this morning on suspicion of race-fixing.'

I can't believe it. I know the Jockey Club and police are always on the lookout for this kind of thing, and understandably clamp down hard on it whenever they find it, but Kieren? None of this fits with the man I know. I'm sure he's innocent and will prove that, but for some people the fact that his name is out there in this context will mean that they automatically assume him to be guilty: no smoke without fire and all that. It's bitterly unfair.

We're racing at Salisbury the following day. Kieren's been bailed, but I don't really expect him to turn up: until he does, that is, with five camera crews and about 50 snappers following every step he takes. He doesn't turn a hair. His sangfroid and mental hardness are off the scale. If that were me I don't think I'd be able to go out in public, let alone go and ride six races in an afternoon. Kieren just shows up like it's no big deal. That's why they call him the assassin: he's ice-cold.

The weighing room's the only place they don't follow him into.

'What time did they come for you?' I ask.

'4.30 yesterday morning,' he replies, as if he's talking about taking an early flight or something. He's just not fazed, not in the slightest. It's extraordinary.

We're both chasing the championship like it's our first, and it's exhausting. Near the end, when I'm seven in front, we have 13 rides on a Saturday, seven at Newmarket and six at Wolverhampton, starting just after lunch and ending at half past nine, with a helicopter ride in between, and then we're due to ride a packed programme at Edinburgh the next day.

'Listen,' I say, 'I'm shattered, you're shattered. If you go to Edinburgh then I have to go too. If you want to carry on till the end, we'll go for it, but if you give in, I'll stop too.'

'My agent's got me those rides, Frankie. I have to go.'

'OK, fine. See you at Stansted in the morning.'

I don't get home till gone midnight, and then I have to get up at seven to catch the flight to Edinburgh. I check in at Stansted Airport and go through security. There's no sign of Kieren, even though we arranged to meet here.

My mobile rings. KIEREN.

'Where are you, mate?' I say.

'Congratulations.'

'Congratulations? Congratulations for what?'

'I'm not going to Edinburgh.'

He ends the call. That's it. He's got me going all the way to Edinburgh before telling me he's just chucked the towel in! Typical Kieren. I laugh. Even when he loses, he has the last laugh.

But that's it. A decade after I first became champion jockey, I've won it for a third time, and in lots of ways this has been the hardest and most satisfying of all: not just because of everything I've been through, but because Kieren's been such a bloody tough opponent.

I thought you'd retired. I thought you'd retired.
Not retired. Champion.

It's the last afternoon of the season at Doncaster. I've finished on 195, with Kieren 15 behind. When Kieren hands me the trophy, I feel like Frankie the jockey rather than Frankie the star. It's a feeling I like.

Catherine and the kids are here to see it. I make a little speech once the champagne has stopped spraying.

'I'd really like to dedicate this championship to my wife, who gave me the push to go out and do it. She set the snowball rolling. I'm glad that she was here today to support me because she was a big part of this championship. My family have been my inspiration. Nine years since my last championship has been a long time.'

It's a loop, I realise, all the way round. Before the crash I was a slave to my job, doing everything to please everybody else. Then I went through recuperation, trying to find happiness again. Then I got a bit lazy. And finally I got back to where I am.

The biggest sacrifice of my life is food. I love it, love it, love it. But I can't have it. Sometimes I'm bad Frankie: I'll have friends over for a barbecue on a Saturday, have a few drinks, nice and relaxing, then on Sunday I'll have a craving for chocolate and eat a couple of the kids' Kinder Surprise eggs. I'll start the weekend at 8 stone, 9 pounds and end it at 9 stone. Nine stone!

So on Monday morning I set my alarm for 5 a.m. I get up, put on my tracksuit, hat, scarf, gloves, raincoat and overcoat, and I get on my treadmill for an hour. Then I get off and go in my sauna. I go in and out, in and out, as long as I can stand it for another hour. At seven o'clock I get back on my scales. I'm 8 st 9 lb. Good Frankie is back!

We live in Barney Curley's old house in Stetchworth. True to his word, he did indeed sell it to me once I'd become champion jockey: in fact, we swapped houses because he wanted to downsize. It's a madhouse of children, animals, mud and noise. My dream is to live in a penthouse with a concierge service down below, no animals, no garden, and a humongous TV which only I can control. I'd flick through every single channel on English Sky and Italian Sky and then start again when that was done. I'd be happy as a pig in shit.

In March 2005 I'm invited to Buckingham Palace for a banquet because the Italian President Carlo Azeglio Ciampi and his wife Franca are on a state visit. All the Beefeaters in the main hall wink at me as I walk past: I bet they're gamblers, most of them, so I hope I've won them some decent cash over the years.

We line up to be presented to the Queen, Prince Philip, and Signor and Signora Ciampi.

'And this is your famous jockey,' says the Queen when I reach the head of the line.

Signor Ciampi raises an eyebrow. 'What kind of music do you play?'

For the 2005 Derby I'm riding Dubawi, who was sired by Dubai Millennium. This would be such a poignant way to break my duck, on the son of the best horse I've ever ridden. We're third favourite at 5/1, and third is where we finish, run out of it by the favourite Motivator.

The wait goes on: by now it's the only big race I haven't won, and it feels like a vital piece missing from my professional jigsaw. Next year, I tell myself. I'll win it next year.

I've been telling myself that since 1992.

At the 2005 St Leger, I ride – and win on – Scorpion. Nothing unusual there, perhaps: except for the fact that Scorpion belongs to Coolmore, Godolphin's arch-rivals.

Technically I've done nothing wrong. Godolphin don't have a runner in the race, so I'm free to take a ride from anyone else who offers me one. But Coolmore …

it's like a Liverpool player being given the day off and going to play for Manchester United. Any other stable, owner or trainer would be fine, but not Coolmore. I can't be black one day and white the next.

In my defence, I don't know half of the politics going on at the time. Only after the race do I find out that, at the annual Keeneland sales in Kentucky, Godolphin decided to boycott all Coolmore horses. They wouldn't buy a single one. There's me at Doncaster giving high fives to all and sundry, and a few days later I'm on the verge of losing my job. I plead innocence to how bad things have got between the two operations, which is true, but I'm left in no doubt that, now I know all about it, this kind of thing can't happen again. I'm not even allowed to speak to anyone from Coolmore on any matter whatsoever, racing or otherwise. In fact, I stop going to Barbados on holiday altogether, just because a lot of the Coolmore people go there. Even if I never saw them, it still wouldn't look good.

I vow that I won't ride for Coolmore again, and I mean it: but I don't know that in seven years' time I'll break that vow, deliberately, and in doing so will set in train a series of events which will threaten everything.

*　*　*

I'm due to ride Authorized in the 2007 Derby, unless Godolphin enter a runner at the last minute and oblige me to ride that instead. Authorized, trained by Peter Chapple-Hyam, is the best horse in the race. The only person who could muck this is up is me. I'm so close. This is the time.

As they say, you make your bed and you lie in it. In the past I've taken the piss out of every jockey, and they can't wait to rip me. Three weeks out I've got Martin Dwyer going, 'Tick-tock, tick-tock,' every time he sees me: 'Poor old Frankie: the time's coming and you're so nervous.' They're tearing me to shreds in the weighing room. Johnny Murtagh says, 'Frankie, listen, I've won three Derbies. How many have you won?' He makes a big fat circle with his thumb and middle finger. 'Are you feeling the pressure?'

They're having a lot of fun. I can't blame them.

I fall at Goodwood. Eight days out from the Derby and I fall. First things first: nothing's broken. I'm bruised and my knee hurts like hell, but that's a jockey's lot. I can ride. That's all that matters.

I ride Authorized in a gallop at Peter's yard. He asks me twice to see if I'm really sure, but funnily enough there's more discomfort when I'm sitting or trotting. When I'm in the jockey's position there's no pain at all.

We gallop over nearly a mile. Authorized is very relaxed and travelling extremely well, clean-winded and light on his feet: then he pulls out for the last two furlongs and finishes really strongly. He's not the best of work horses, so this is really pleasing.

It's Sunday. I'm on my way to the races when Ray rings.

'Mate, Sheikh Mohammed's released you for the Derby. You can ride Authorized.'

I just scream, and then I scream again, even louder.

It's a weight off my mind: but equally now I know I have to deliver, now I've got to go out there and do it. There have only been about four odds-on shots in the Derby in the last 50 years, so to have a ride on a horse like Authorized is pretty special. Even the great horses I've ridden in the Derby all had question marks about them: Dubai Millennium was a doubtful stayer, Cape Verdi was a filly taking on the colts.

It doesn't matter which corner I turn or which shop I go into: everybody's wishing me the best of luck, and I don't think I've ever been in such a sustained and intense media spotlight before a race. The whole story has captured people's imagination: not just the horse, but also whether I can win after so long trying.

* * *

Michael Hills's dog up the road bites me. Rocco, only just three, suffers an asthma attack the night before the Derby. It all seems to be conspiring against me. *Not now. Not this time. Please.*

My heart's thudding like an entire brass band, and I can't sleep. I don't like taking stuff to make me nod off, and I don't normally need to, but I don't want to ride the Derby on no sleep. So I take half a herbal sleeping pill.

There are other races on the card before the big one. I'm caught near the finish on Bespoke Boy in the Woodcote Stakes, I finish second on the favourite Blue Ksar in the Diomed Stakes after getting in a tangle with one of the other horses' discarded blindfolds, and then in the Dash sprint I come in seventh on the joint favourite Bond City. I always try to give everything in every race I ride, but I wouldn't be human if I didn't have half a mind on the Derby later this afternoon.

I haven't won since I fell off at Goodwood last week: not a single race, anywhere.

'He'll have to sharpen up, Dettori, otherwise he'll win nothing,' says one punter by the winner's enclosure.

Sometimes if you win too much too early you don't finish well. At least that's what I tell myself.

Aidan O'Brien has eight runners in the race. The stewards call those eight jockeys in before the race and remind them that team riding is strictly prohibited. I'm not bothered one way or the other. If Authorized runs as well as he can and I ride as well as I can, then we should be untouchable.

If. If. If.

We've drifted to 5/4, so we won't start odds-on. Again, I'm not bothered. How we start isn't the issue: it's where we finish.

Peter and I discuss tactics. 'Don't worry about position for the first mile,' he says. 'But whatever you do, get the horse relaxed. If he's relaxed, he'll blow the rest away.'

'OK.'

'Most of all, Frankie, do one thing.'

'What's that?'

'Ride it like you own it.'

As we leave the weighing room, I squeeze Pat Smullen's neck and wish him luck. There are punters all around, never short of an opinion. 'He's going to blow it again.' 'He's not that good, you know. Lester won it nine times, first as an 18-year-old.'

I tune them all out and canter Authorized up to the start.

This is it. If I'm ever going to win it, it's surely now. I smile to myself. Beyond the nerves there's a perverse sort of pleasure too: this is why I do what I do, for moments like this, because pressure is only the shadow of great opportunity. A 15-year quest for a race which lasts 150 seconds.

We're sprung from the stalls and start the long climb. I hang back, wanting to be able to watch the race unfold in front of me and not risk getting boxed in. As we come round Tattenham Corner and start running downhill, I can see all nine horses in front of me. I'm a little further back than I want, but I have a proper look, checking them out one by one. *Nah*, I think, *these guys are all cooked. I've got them beat.* I look behind and see daylight between me and the other seven.

I hear the words of two men in my head.

Lester first: *Don't let Derby fever get to you. Ride the horse, not the race.*

Then Dad. *Keep it simple. Don't improvise, invent or try to be clever. Just follow the rest, get a nice run, smooth and clear, and win. You've got the best horse.*

Three furlongs out I know I'm going to win, and for a moment I swear my heart stops beating. I see the racetrack like a green strip, a glorious verdant runway. I don't take my eyes off it. It's like looking down a funnel, with everything else a blur except that narrow strip of grass. I don't see the crowds or the stands, I don't even really see the other runners. Just this green strip, beckoning me forward.

This is it, the moment I've been waiting for. For 15 years I've dreamt of this. I had it 12 years ago for literally a second, when Tamure hit the front only for Lammtarra to blow right past us. But no one's coming past us now.

I hit the front with just over a furlong left. *Don't do anything fancy, don't fall off, keep the horse going to the line.* It seems to take for ever: time slowing down so I can savour it, but also I just want the line to get here. It's all so smooth, like an oil painting.

I scream as I cross the line. It's not a simple scream of triumph, but one which contains many other things too: the pain of so many losses, the anguish of hopes extinguished year after year after year, the fear that I might have blown this last, best chance, and most of all the sheer relief that I haven't. The final piece of the jigsaw's in place: the sole blemish on my career has gone.

I hear the other jockeys shouting their congratulations, but they seem distant and muffled.

In the unsaddling enclosure, I leap onto the presentation table. 'I love you all,' I yell. 'Come on, me.'

Thirty-one years ago, Dad rode Wollow here. They'd won the 2000 Guineas a few weeks before and were 11/10 favourites, but only finished fifth. Dad wept tears of disappointment that day: now he weeps tears of joy.

After hours of interviews and autographs the initial high has worn off, and in its place comes a crashing tiredness but also a profound satisfaction. I can happily retire – not now, but one day – and be able to tell my children that I won the Derby, the Arc, the King George, every Classic, and I've been champion jockey. I've conquered everything in my sport. I want to do more, of course, but I've ticked off all the big ones.

On the way back to Newmarket, I tell the pilot to fly low over Stetchworth so I can wake everyone up. I run around knocking on everyone's door, telling them to join me in the pub. At one in the morning I'm trying to speak to Peter, but I can't get any words out. He kicks me into the back of a taxi and says, 'You're riding the French Derby today, so go and get some sleep.'

God knows what time it is, and I'm three sheets to the wind, but I still hang my clothes up neatly. I always do. It cracks Catherine up something rotten. 'You're so anal,' she says, crying with laughter.

Twelve hours later I win the French Derby on Lawman. The horse knows I'm in a winning mood. It's incredible. With so much adrenaline pumping, I feel brand new.

When I get home, I find a whole bunch of flowers from Kieren. I ring and ask, 'What are the flowers about? Do you fancy my missus?' He just laughs, but I really appreciate the gesture. He's won the Derby three times, so he knows what a big deal it is.

A few days after the Derby, Brough Scott writes something in the *Guardian* which means a lot to me:

Having closely watched all the great riders of the last half-century I would say there are aspects in which Frankie is outgunned by each of them.

But with Frankie we are not talking about one particular skill or some magic moment of strategic inspiration, we are acknowledging the whole set. He is a more flowing rider than Richards, stronger than Shoemaker, more varied than Breasley, more travelled than Saint-Martin, better balanced than either Piggott or Kieren Fallon.

That's the physical aspect but in racing it is the horse that does the running so the real key to jockeyship is the strategic decisions taken by the man behind the mane. Many more races are lost because of faulty judgment as in race passage or tempo than ever are by muscular machinations in the saddle. At 36, with his technique refined, his energy retained and his success registered in every racing parish, Dettori is better equipped for the big occasion than anyone else in a helmet.

'Here,' Dad says. 'I've got something for you.'

I recognise the box even before he gives it to me. The Piaget watch he promised me as a kid if I ever won the Derby.

'Open it,' he says.

I do. I lift the watch out as though it's the Koh-i-Noor diamond – which to me it pretty much is – and I see that he's had the back engraved:

LANFRANCO DETTORI
AUTHORIZED
EPSOM DERBY
SATURDAY 2 JUNE 2007.

I hug him. He only ever brought the watch out once a year, and I know that I won't even do that. I'll never wear it. That watch has been so big in my life that I'm scared to wear it. To me it's a symbol of so much. It's not just a reward for winning a race or a marker of growing up. It reminds me where I came from and what I have.

5

KNOCKDOWN

Royal Ascot in 2009 opens with the Queen Anne Stakes, and Godolphin have got two runners in it: Gladiatorus, the best colt in the world who's the 9/4 favourite, and Alexandros at 13/2. So far so good, except for one thing: I'm on Alexandros.

I've been with Godolphin for 15 years, and in that time I can count on the fingers of one hand the amount of times I've ridden a second-string horse in a major race. There's logic behind the decision, of course: there always is with Godolphin. I've ridden Alexandros for eight of his last 10 races, while Ahmed Ajtebi, an apprentice who used to be a camel jockey in the UAE, rode Gladiatorus for two of his three victories in Dubai earlier this year, including the £2 million Dubai Duty Free. We both know our horses well and each other's hardly at all: the only time I've ever ridden Gladiatorus was in Italy two years ago, when he was under different ownership.

As it is, the Queen Anne is a bust for both of us. I know even before we get to the starting stalls that Alexandros isn't up for it, and when in the finishing straight it's clear he's well beaten I ease him right back and save him for another day. Ahmed's sixth and I'm eighth.

There's a bit of gossip that Ahmed got the ride instead of me. He's a talented jockey on his way up the ladder, but he's also inexperienced. I tune it out. As I said, it was a perfectly logical decision. I've been Godolphin's number one rider ever since I joined them, but I know how high their standards are, and I know too that as a jockey you're only ever as good as your next race, let alone your last one.

'We are not having a second jockey,' Simon tells the press, 'but we will be putting Ahmed up from time to time, the same as we will be looking for the best available for lots of our horses when Frankie is unavailable. In no way does this affect Frankie's role.'

I don't have to chase anything I don't want to any more. I just have to chase what I enjoy. The only thing I enjoy now is riding the big meetings and the big weekends. I've cut out a lot of the nonsense races, when I'm just turning up to show people I'm there. I've gone beyond that now. I don't enjoy riding in the nine o'clock at

Kempton, so why bother doing it? I'm a much happier person, but I'm also a better jockey as well. I'm less tired, more focused, and when I go racing it's because I want to, and I want to win.

I'm not interested in the championship. I'm not interested in statistics. I'm only interested in big winners. Since that brutal 195-winner championship season in 2004, I've finished 15th, fifth, 17th and 29th in terms of winners: but if the championship were based on prize money, I'd have finished 10th, first, first and second over the same period. I go for the big pots or not at all. I'm riding as well as I ever have, but on my own terms.

Godolphin announce that they'll split their string between two trainers in Newmarket for the 2010 season, with Mahmood al Zarooni and Saeed bin Suroor dividing the horses between them in separate stables. Mahmood has been Saeed's assistant for a year or so, so he knows the set-up. Technically both Ahmed and I can ride for either trainer and flip-flop between stables, but primarily Ahmed will ride for Mahmood while I'll stay with Saeed. So far as I'm concerned, it's business as usual and won't affect me too much.

*   *   *

Tony McCoy finally wins the Grand National on Don't Push It, at the 15th time of asking – exactly the same number of times it took me to win the Derby, so if anyone knows how he must be feeling it's me. I'm so made up for him when he wins: I have a big lump in my throat, and it's all I can do not to cry. In some ways his achievement is even bigger than mine, as so much more can go wrong in a four-mile 30-fence race than it can in a mile-and-a-half flat race. For Tony, who's rewritten every record under the sun over jumps, it would have hurt like hell to finish his career without winning the Grand National. I speak to him that night, and the emotions I can hear in his voice are exactly the same as mine were three years ago when I crossed the line first at Epsom on Authorized: joy, relief and a deep satisfaction.

I win the 2011 1000 Guineas on Blue Bunting, one of Mahmood's horses. That evening, I invite practically everyone I know round for a drink. The house doors are wide open, the gates are wide open, it's a free-for-all: there are 200 people here, easily.

The next morning I wake up to absolute carnage: bottles everywhere, ashtrays overflowing, a hangover the size of Heathrow, and no sign of our wire-haired dachshund Scrooby. I look everywhere for her – all around the house, the garden, the paddocks, the stables, everywhere. No sign. By the time I get back inside the house, I see I've got a voicemail. It's Carolyn Warren, whose husband John is the Queen's racing manager. I ring her back.

'I've got Scrooby,' she says. 'Found her in the street and rang the number on her collar. She's absolutely fine.'

'Great,' I say. 'I'll come over.'

'Well, it'll have to be later, as we're going to Sandringham now.'

'As you do.'

She laughs. 'We're going to pick up the Queen, as she wants to watch Carlton House work on the gallops.' Carlton House is Her Majesty's big hope for the Derby next month. 'We'll be done by early evening, so come round at about seven and you can say hi to Her Majesty and pick up Scrooby.'

Sounds like a plan. I lean out of the window and yell across to the stables, where Catherine's mucking the ponies out. 'I've found the dog!'

'Who's got her?'

'The Queen.'

She laughs, gives me a V-sign, shakes her head at my unending idiocy, and goes back to the mucking out.

Later that day I put on a suit, get Ella to put on a nice dress, and go round to John and Carolyn's to pick

Scrooby up. I bow to the Queen – Lord Carnarvon would be proud of me – and, as we chat about Carlton House's chances, I see Scrooby run towards Ella, stop, and wee on the carpet in excitement. Ella instantly stands on the puddle to try and hide it.

I'm desperately trying to concentrate on how Carlton House might run at the Dante Stakes in 10 days' time and how this will be Her Majesty's 10th attempt at winning the Derby. Her horses have never been closer than second, and that was in her Coronation year of 1953. It puts my 15-year wait before Authorized into perspective. And all I can think about is how my dog's just wee'd everywhere in the Queen's presence. Maybe there's a thirteenth-century treason law against this still on the statute books and I'll get carted off to the Tower of London.

I ride Blue Bunting again in the Oaks, and we're favourite at 9/4, but any chance of repeating the 1000 Guineas success goes when I mess up my tactics. Johnny Murtagh takes up the lead on Dancing Rain almost from the start, and we run the first mile at a steady pace. I'm back in midfield and think I have everything covered, but when Dancing Rain ups the pace off the front in the final straight I'm trapped behind the horses ahead of me and too far off the pace. I barge my way to the outside and ask Blue Bunting to give me everything he's got, but I've left him too much to do. When I realise he's beaten I'm in third, and I drop my hands and, unforgivably, let William Buick on Izzi Top get past me right at the line. Anyone who had me each way will be furious, and rightly so.

These things happen, even to the best, and when it comes to riding big races I'm exceptional, I know I am. No jockey is an automaton capable of riding at his best every time. But it makes me angry with myself that after so long in the game I should still be making such rookie errors.

At the Derby 24 hours later I'm on Ocean War, and it's not my day: we finish 11th out of 13. It's not the Queen's day either, with Carlton House run out of it at the finish and beaten into third. But it is very much the young French jockey Mickaël Barzalona's day. He's stone last on Pour Moi from the stalls all the way to the start of the home straight, but he picks off the field one by one, including five in the last furlong alone, until there's just Treasure Beach ahead with the line coming fast.

It's only in the last three strides that Pour Moi gets his nose in front, and even then it's still desperately close, but Mickaël is standing up in his irons, saluting the crowd even before they cross the line. That's the kind of confidence only the very best jockeys have, and it comes from the ability to see things happening before everyone else does and to slow time down so that you can do more in a given second or two than anyone else can.

The stewards warn Mickaël about 'the timing and manner of his celebration', but the crowd love it. He's only 19, he's a showman and crowd-pleaser, and he rides horses as though he was born to it. Now, who does that remind you of?

Godolphin announce that for the 2012 season, with around 350 horses between Saeed and Mahmood, they'll be employing both Mickaël and Silvestre de Sousa. A Frenchman, a Brazilian and an Italian ... it sounds like the opening of a joke.

But if so, it's not one that I find particularly funny. The talk is of Godolphin planning ahead for when I retire, as if the timing of that retirement is going to be my decision, my decision alone, and not take place for a while yet. 'Frankie's got plenty of years left in him,' Simon tells the press. 'I know he's said publicly that he wants to keep going for at least another five years. So long as he's healthy and fit, I don't see why he wouldn't continue riding for us. And in five or 10 years' time these other jockeys will have gained some of the experience that Frankie's got. We are a big stable: a little short on quality just now, but quantity is not an issue. It's not like there's going to be a pecking order.' Most of the reporters take that as meaning I'll still be number one with Mickaël and Silvestre sharing the duties as number two.

It all sounds reasonable enough, and in many ways it is. Simon's a good guy, I get on well with him, and like everyone else in the operation he's looking only at what's best for Godolphin as a whole. Mickaël and Silvestre are good jockeys and nice young lads whom I like a lot. But the whole idea behind splitting the Godolphin operation into two trainers was that each trainer would have a principal retained jockey: it started out with Saeed and me alongside Mahmood and Ahmed. Now there are three jockeys, and even with my maths I know that three into two doesn't go. I haven't got this far without knowing which way the wind is blowing, and on that wind I can sense the vultures beginning to circle.

Mickaël wins the Dubai World Cup on the 20/1 outsider Monterosso, kicking clear halfway down the straight and winning by three lengths. He's now won the world's most famous flat race and its richest too, both before his 21st birthday. He's the coming man, the rising star, the golden boy, and no mistake, if he keeps on going at this rate he's going to be one of the richest and most famous riders in the world.

Godolphin's big Derby hope is Mandaean, but Mickaël rode him at the Dante Stakes and he'll keep that ride. We don't have any other likely runners. Aidan O'Brien will have a few for Coolmore, but of course I can't ride for him, not after what happened at the St Leger seven years ago. It's going to be a very tight race this year, and all the other fancied horses are organised with their own jockeys and tied to their own stables, so they're not going to be taking their own jockeys off just to put me on. Apart from 2000, when I'd just had the plane crash, this is going to be the first Derby I've missed since 1992. Two decades in the race I value above all others, and I can't even get a ride. This is not good. This is not good at all.

As it is, Mandaean is scratched, so there'll be no Godolphin runner at all in the Derby. But there will be one in the Oaks the day before, Kailani, and Mickaël gets the nod there. I haven't missed an Oaks since 1991, again apart from 2000.

'Rides will be split across the board,' Simon tells the press. 'The three jockeys will all get equal opportunities. Frankie has to share the cake and he understands that.

We brought in two new, young jockeys and it's obviously important to give them opportunities. For years Frankie was our only retained jockey. We had other people who would regularly ride for us but it was an informal arrangement. These two jockeys are formally retained. I thought we made it reasonably clear at the time that, if any one of them struck up a winning combination with a certain horse, the chances are they are going to stay on that horse. Certainly that's Frankie's understanding of the situation.'

I understand all right. I'm officially no longer number one. I understand it and I don't like it, not one little bit. Simon's words from a few months before come back to me: *It's not like there's going to be a pecking order.* Too right there's not.

I watch the Oaks from the weighing room at Epsom. On Derby Day I'm not even at the course: I'm at Haydock, where I ride three races and finish fifth, eighth and last. I can feel people looking at me with a mixture of curiosity and pity. The Derby without Frankie feels like Hamlet without the Prince, to me at least. I'm going through the motions: miles from where I want to be, in every sense.

It's like being Ronaldo and always sitting on the bench. Basically, I'm being paid not to ride. This isn't right. This is all happening in front of me, but I can't say anything. I've still got a lot more to give, and I'm not having somebody else be in front of me when I'm more than good enough to hold my own. But the money's good, and I've been here so long, maybe this is just a blip that will sort itself out, so I keep my mouth shut.

For now.

Some journalists liken it to a nature documentary, with the young buck looking to prove himself an alpha male by besting the old stag and driving him away to the mountains. In the Queen Anne, Mickaël's on Helmet for Godolphin, so I ride Worthadd for Sir Mark Prescott. It's a strange feeling, being in a Group 1 race against a rider in Godolphin blue without wearing it myself: almost as though there's been a mix-up with the valets and I've gone out in the wrong colours. Since Frankel's in the race neither of us have a chance, but that's immaterial. It's a very visible sign of the changing of the guard. This isn't any old course: this is Ascot, pretty much my home turf, scene of my finest hour, and if I'm not Godolphin's automatic top rider in the biggest races here then you know things aren't how they used to be.

The Gold Cup's in two days' time. Godolphin are running two horses, Colour Vision and Opinion Poll.

'You choose, Frankie,' says Sheikh Mohammed.

Even this seems designed to put me in a difficult position. If I lose, I won't be able to say they gave me the inferior horse. I'd better get this right.

The Gold Cup is two and a half miles, long for a flat race, and there's rain forecast between now and then, so the going will be good to soft. Staying power will count for a lot, so I choose the horse which I think has the better stamina.

'Colour Vision,' I say.

I can't remember the last time I wanted to win a race this badly. The 2007 Derby, perhaps. Five years ago. Usually it's the jockeys in other colours who provide the biggest rivalry, and of course now there's the extra frisson when I ride against any Coolmore horses, but going head to head with Mickaël adds yet another layer of spice. It's not just that I want to win: I *need* to win, to prove to Sheikh Mohammed, Saeed, Mahmood, Mickaël and most of all myself that I'm still top dog and not going anywhere for a while. I may not be riding quite for my life, but I feel certainly as though I'm riding for my career.

I settle Colour Vision in near the front of the field, never lower than third. Mickaël's behind me, but for most of the time I can't see him. *Don't worry about him. Ride your own race.* The pace is steady for much of the running, but as we get into the last few furlongs the ratchet starts to turn and we see who's got it and who hasn't.

Two furlongs left. Gulf of Naples has led almost from the start, but now I sweep past – and out of nowhere Mickaël comes alongside me! Here we go. It's on.

A furlong out and we're neck and neck, so close that the horses bump and bounce off each other as I edge left, away from the riders on my inside. Mickaël and me: two jockeys, dressed identically, driving their horses on. At stake is the Gold Cup and so, so much more.

Mickaël edges Opinion Poll ahead: a nose, if that.

No way. No fucking way.

Give me what you've got, I ask Colour Vision. *Give me everything you've got, and I'll match it.*

We edge up back alongside Opinion Poll. I can hear the crowd going wild. This is half race, half prize-fight, and it's going to come down simply to who wants it more.

He can't possibly want it more than I do. He can't.

Still I drive Colour Vision for all he's worth. We begin to edge ahead. Less than a hundred yards to go and I know we have it. In the last strides we're in command, and we flash across the line half a length up.

I punch the air. That felt special: very, very special.

The stewards hold a brief inquiry into the coming together just inside the furlong marker, but I know there's nothing in it: there was no intent from either rider, neither horse was impeded, but these things happen a dozen times every race. It's only when you're eyeballs out in the last strides that it might make a difference.

The press ask me whether the victory has reaffirmed my status as number one. How can I answer that directly? The choice isn't mine to make. I'm as diplomatic as I can be: 'I had a very hard decision to make, as they are both great, tough horses. It's been a very hard week and I'm delighted for the team. Me and Mickaël are good friends, but when you're there you want to win. You're only as good as the last winner you rode, though. Now I have to do it again.'

But will I get the chance?

When it was Ahmed and me, he was mainly with Mahmood and I was with Saeed. But now there are three of us, that old distinction has gone. I've got much more to do with Mahmood than I did, which would be fine were it not for one thing: he doesn't rate me.

He makes that very clear. He never says so outright, of course, but he doesn't need to. He gives the best rides to Mickaël, not just once but again and again: by the end of the season Mickaël will have ridden almost three times as many races for him as I will.

I'm contracted as first jockey, but I'm not riding all the best horses. It's a gradual process, nothing as simple as me being jocked off for ever and ever: a second-string horse here, another second-string horse there, until one day I realise I'm losing out on the prime rides way more often than not, and every time I see a horse win without me it's like a kick in the balls.

I'm never given an explanation. I have to accept it, even though I don't know the reasons. I'm not sleeping at night, Catherine and I are arguing. But there's always this thought: *Maybe I'll be all right next week, maybe I'll be back in favour.*

But the weeks go by and things keep on getting worse. My head is wrecked, absolutely wrecked. I can't take it much longer.

Early in September I win the Irish Champion Stakes in Leopardstown, but it doesn't really improve my mood. When I get back home I have a few people round. The booze is flowing, I'm feeling low and frustrated and angry, and I want to blot out all the shit that's going on in my head and my life.

Someone's chopping up a few lines of coke.

I shouldn't. We get randomly drug tested now and then, and cocaine shows up the same as any other drug. But how unlucky would I be to get pinged? Also: it's late, I'm drunk, I'm pissed off, my career's on the skids, and fundamentally I don't care.

I remember the name of the horse I rode to victory earlier today: Snow Fairy. I laugh. Could it be any more appropriate? That has to be a sign, no?

Fuck it. I take a rolled-up £20 note, bend my head to the table and snort a line. And then another, and another, and another.

It's 9 a.m. before I go to bed, and when I wake up I've got the fear big time. What was I doing? It wasn't just a single line I took, either: I got really stuck in.

I drink pints of water to try to flush it out of my system. I've got the week off before the St Leger, so I don't have to worry about every last pound the water will put on: I can get rid of those over the coming days. A week is as long as cocaine usually stays in the system, at least in enough quantities to be detectable. But it stays in longer if the person is dehydrated, and every jockey is dehydrated: that's how we keep our weight down.

In any situation like this it takes just one moment to put it all into perspective and make me face up to things once and for all. Barney asking me over a game of snooker how serious I was about being a jockey, Thomas asking me how long I'd been retired. A moment which rams home something very simple: this isn't going to go away, so what are you going to do about it? And that moment here is the St Leger.

Godolphin only have one runner in the St Leger: Encke, who finished second last year. He's a 25/1 outsider, having lost at Goodwood and York recently: but still, he's the only entrant we have, and the St Leger is my turf. I've won it five times, including three out of the past seven. I know this course like the back of my hand, and I get horses to run at their best here. This ride should be mine every day of the week and twice on Sunday.

They give it to Mickaël.

It's Sheikh Mohammed's choice, like everything here, but Mahmood has campaigned so hard for Mickaël that the decision was practically made already. As far as I'm concerned it's pretty much the last straw. They could hardly be making it clearer if they tried. If I'm not number one rider for Godolphin here at the St Leger, I'm not number one for them anywhere: and if I'm not number one, when I'm still riding as well as I ever have, then why am I bothering in the first place? It's an insult to me and my career. I'm 42 years old, and I'm not having it. *If you want to fire me, fire me. I'm big and ugly enough to take it. But don't insult me with this limbo.*

That writing on the wall is practically 10-foot-high neon letters now.

I ride Michelangelo for John. He knows I'm not my usual sunny self: he also knows how sweet it would be to win this one, not just as a gigantic middle finger to Godolphin, but also because it was 16 years ago that I won on Shantou here and gave him his first Classic win.

The situation between Godolphin and me isn't the only subplot to this race. Camelot, trained by Aidan O'Brien and ridden by his son Joseph, has already won the 2000 Guineas and the Derby, so today he's going for the Triple Crown, last done 42 years ago – the year I was born – by Nijinsky and Lester. So victory for any of us – Joseph, Mickaël or me – will mean more than just winning a Classic.

We three sit in the middle of the field for the first half of the race, shadowing each other: Mickaël ahead of me, me ahead of Joseph. With three furlongs to go, Joseph is first to move, coming up the inside on the rails. He can't get through there, so he comes right, almost on top of me. But Mickaël has first run on both of us, and with two furlongs to go he has three lengths and daylight on the entire field. Joseph goes after him but hasn't got enough track left to hunt him down, and I have to settle for third.

I look like thunder afterwards, and even that's a lot sunnier than I feel inside.

The hell with them. The hell with them all.

I ride on Arc trials day at Longchamp the next day.

Four races. Three placings. No wins.

And one drug test.

I work out the timeline as I pee into the bottle. It was just over a week ago that I took the cocaine. It's going to be touch and go. And I've got a bad feeling about it. Everything else in my life is going wrong, so why not this? Deep down, in those places we call superstition and instinct, I know that this isn't going to be good.

Every day after that test I'm walking on eggshells. Every day I wait for a letter – I feel sure they'll send me a letter rather than an email or doing it by phone: they're French, they'll have good manners at least – and every day that the post comes and there's nothing from them I let myself relax a bit until the next morning, when it all starts again. But how long will it go on for? What's the period after which no news is good news?

Mickaël is riding Masterstroke for Godolphin in the Arc. Camelot is favourite, but Joseph's too heavy to make the weight.

Michael Tabor, one of Britain's richest men and co-owner of Camelot, phones me.

'Frankie, do you want to ride Camelot in the Arc?'

I almost yelp in delight. It's too good a chance to pass up. It's the perfect storm, everything I've wanted, like winning the lottery. In a single stroke I feel wanted again; I have the chance to show Godolphin what they're missing and I can finally see a way out of the job. This will force the issue into the open, one way or another: and it needs forcing, because another six months here and I'll end up in the Priory for sure. I'm done in, absolutely done in. This is my ticket out, and I grab it like a drowning man grabs a lifebuoy.

I'm not legally in breach of my contract. If I'm not asked to ride for Godolphin in a given race then I can take any other ride I choose. But opting for Camelot, and Coolmore, is more or less a declaration of war. I know it, they know it, everyone in racing knows it. Seven years ago, when I rode Scorpion for Coolmore in the St Leger, I only just got away with it, and that was because I genuinely didn't know the extent of the politics and animosity between the two stables. I've got no such excuse now, and nor do I claim one. Last time I was stupid and didn't know what I was doing. This time I'm angry and know exactly what I'm doing.

'You're damn right I want to ride Camelot,' I reply.

'You know what's going to happen if you do?'
'I know exactly. That's why I want to ride him.'

The decision sets press tongues wagging. Some people write that I might be about to retire, or join Coolmore, or perhaps sign with one of the new Qatari owners getting in on the racing scene. Few people seem to believe that I've just had enough and have no back-up plan. The end of the road for me, or at least the beginning of the end? Or maybe a new beginning, in every way?

I speak to the two people I trust more than any other, Catherine and Dad. I lay out my choices to them. I'm 42, I've got financial security at Godolphin, and with five kids, that's an important consideration. It's a big call. A very big call. Either I stay put and get humiliated in front of everyone for the rest of my career until I decide to retire, or I make a stand, go my own way and take my chances. And when I put it like that, it comes down to something very simple: which way leaves me with my pride? I've spent 20 years doing what I do, I'm damn good at it, and I'm proud of that. I can't buy pride, and I can't put a price on it either. How much is rich? How do I measure wealth? Because true wealth isn't just financial. And if the choice is between being kicked in the balls every day for money or ending up with nothing, then I'd rather end up with nothing. I honestly would.

Catherine and Dad both say the same thing: at the end of the day this has to be your call, but we'll support you whatever you do.

One Monday morning, I walk into Simon's office.

'I want to leave,' I say. No messing about, I get straight to the point.

'Are you mad?'

'No, I'm not mad. I just can't take it any more. I've been sidelined time and again, and no one's given me any explanation, no one's had the decency to sit down and discuss things with me. I can't get near anyone to talk to them. I've still got a few years left, so I'd rather take a chance on my own and be happy in my rocking chair one day than just sitting around being humiliated in front of the world. I don't deserve that. I don't want to stop my career and think I should have done this, I should have done that. If I'm going to regret something I'd rather it was something I've done rather than something I haven't. It may backfire, but this way I'll live with myself when it does. I don't want to insult Sheikh Mohammed, because he's been so good to me these past 18 years, so you write the press release, you frame it as you like. Blame me if you want, I don't care. But I'm done here.'

We agree that I'll stay till the end of the season. There's not that much of it left as it is, and the only big races I have are the Breeders' Cup and the Melbourne Cup.

Godolphin announce that my retainer won't be renewed for next season by mutual agreement. They say that they won't hire a third jockey: Mickaël will ride mostly for Mahmood while Silvestre teams up with Saeed. At the start of the year they were talking about how they needed three jockeys to cover the number of horses, now that no longer seems to be the case.

I put out my own statement. 'I have had 18 wonderful years. Godolphin have been a major part of everything I have achieved in racing, and I have loved every minute of it. I feel the time has come for a change. My position in the stable has changed a little bit and I need a new challenge. Sheikh Mohammed has been an unbelievable boss to me. He had the confidence to take me on board when I was young and we smashed every record together. I will be forever grateful to him for everything he has done for me and for my family.'

All of which is true: but as ever with these things, it's what I don't say which is just as important as what I do.

* * *

A few days later, a letter arrives from France, recorded delivery. France Galop, it says on the envelope.

Here we go.

I open it. My eyes go immediately to the key phrases. 'Failed a drugs test.' 'Positive for metabolites of cocaine.'

That's it. Busted. This time last year I had a great job and a great career. Now I've got no job and, when this comes out, no career either.

I've only got myself to blame. I can't blame anyone else. It's Sod's Law: I did the wrong thing at the wrong time, and I got tested. If you play with fire you're going to get burned.

I tell the handful of people I need to tell: Catherine, Pete, my dad. The last one is the hardest, just as it was 19 years ago when he came with me to Marylebone police station to receive my caution. He was old-fashioned then, he's old-fashioned now: he'll always be old-fashioned. He thinks that taking cocaine even once means I'm on the fast track to addiction and need to check myself into the Priory immediately.

'Dad, the Priory's where I'd have ended up if I'd stayed at Godolphin, not for any other reason. Listen, I made a mistake. I was depressed. Let's move on.'

I swear them all to secrecy, not that they'd tell anybody anyway.

'You have to come with me to California and Australia,' I tell Catherine. 'I can't do them by myself, not now.'

The Breeders' Cup is at Santa Anita. Five thousand miles in a plane with all that guilt squatting low and heavy on my shoulders. No matter how far I go, I can't outrun it. I go from track to hotel and back again, not going out even once despite all the people and the parties there. I'm totally paranoid, wired and on edge the whole time. I lock myself in my room until it's time to do it all over again the next day. Thank God I've got Catherine with me, or who knows what I might do? I don't win anything, and even if I did, I wouldn't feel much like celebrating – me, king of the flying dismount, who normally loves nothing more than the roar of the crowd and the champagne sprays in the winner's enclosure.

From there we go straight to Australia for the Melbourne Cup. In terms of the effect it has on the nation as a whole, the Melbourne Cup is unparalleled. It's an integral part of Australian popular culture. Even the Derby or the Arc – even the Grand National, come to think of it – can't hold a candle to the Melbourne Cup. Everyone, and I mean everyone, stops to watch or listen to the Melbourne Cup. That's just the way it is for

Australians. It's become a part of Australian popular culture. It's a public holiday in Victoria, and may as well be everywhere else. You want to rob a bank in Australia? Do it at 3.01 p.m. on the first Tuesday in November: no one will stop you.

Catherine's mum is from Australia and her dad's from New Zealand, so every year I get bombarded with texts from her relatives saying, 'Come on, Frankie, this is your time!' It's just about the only big race I haven't won – I've been second three times – and God, it would be so, so good to win it as my farewell to Godolphin, one last hurrah to show them what they've lost.

I finish twelfth.

I'm walking down the steps at Flemington racecourse when a wave of sadness, shocking in its suddenness, hits me. *This is it*, I think. *Any moment now it's all going to be made public and I'll be out, six months minimum: that's the tariff for this kind of offence. And after that, who knows?*

I look around, trying to soak it all in, in case I never see it again.

I want to tell Sheikh Mohammed before the news comes out. He deserves to hear it from me in person: it may well embarrass him to be associated with it, even tangentially, and I'm man enough to want to look him in the eye rather than let him find out via the news. I also want to thank him in person for the 18 years we had together, because I really meant that bit in my statement. They were really great years. Well, 17 of them were. Maybe 17 and a half.

I stop in Dubai on the way back from Melbourne, check into the Emirates Towers, and try to see him. No chance. Every door is shut. I've spent several months here every year for 18 years, so I know the set-up like the back of my hand and I know who to talk to, but even so. The people I can get hold of say they'll do what they can, but I never hear back from them. There are others who never answer the phone to me in the first place. Someone like Sheikh Mohammed has layers and layers of people around him: I can't simply amble in and shoot the breeze with him. Every minute of his time is accounted for. I don't even know whether he knows I'm here.

I stay for almost a week. It's the first time I've been here since parting company with Godolphin, and it's strange: the place is still the same, but it seems different. Or maybe it's me who's changed.

I'm watching Sky News in the hotel one day, and there I am, front and centre. First headline: Frankie Dettori fails drug test and is suspended from riding pending an inquiry. Second headline: President Obama elected for second term. Third headline: war in Syria. I don't know what the world's come to. I just failed a drugs test. I didn't kill anyone. I'm not proud of what I've done, but to be lead item ahead of the most powerful man in the world and an actual war? Come on.

Catherine and I sit the kids down and tell them. Dad's made a mistake, he took some bad stuff he shouldn't have, and he'll probably not be allowed to ride. They take it pretty well, all things considering, as they're too young to really understand what this is all about. Leo's the eldest and he's only just 13.

The press camp outside our house for a week. A week! What are they expecting me to do? And more to the point, isn't there any other news in the world?

Whenever I want to leave the house I have to get in the car in the garage, lie down in the footwell, get covered by a blanket, and then Catherine or someone else drives the car and pretends I'm not inside. The kids find this *hilarious*.

But they're being bullied at school because of what I've done: not all of them, and not all the time, but even one incident for one of them is too much for me. I'm not going to have them made unhappy because of something that isn't their fault.

'Listen,' I say to Catherine, 'why don't we just take them out of school for a term? We hardly ever get any time together as a family, as I'm always off riding. Now I'm going to be around 24/7. Let's make the most of this. Let's go round the world. We've got the time, we've got the money, they're the perfect age for it. We're never going to get this chance again. Next time will be when I retire, and by then the kids will think that going on holiday with their boring square parents is a fate worse than death. Let's make a positive thing out of a bad thing. Besides, I don't want to see anyone round here.'

If people want to see me as a role model then that's on them and not me. There are lots of things I do which I think show a good example – I work hard, I keep refining my craft, I stand up for myself – but there are lots of other things which people might find harder to deal with. I'm expressive, I'm complicated, I've made mistakes which have been magnified a hundred times by being in the public eye. And this is the most public of them all.

The medical committee of France Galop, the French equivalent of the British Horseracing Authority, hold the inquiry in Paris. I'm smuggled in the back way to avoid the photographers: if I never see another camera lens again after the past few weeks, it'll be too soon.

I decide that honesty is the best policy. I don't try to weasel out of it or claim that I didn't know what I was

All the family together in Dubai on holiday, 2016.
From left to right, we have me, Tallula, Mia, Rocco,
Catherine, Ella and Leo.

My first day back at the races in Ascot after the plane crash, 2000. I was desperate to ride the brilliant Dubai Millennium that day but had to watch from the grandstand.

Signorina Cattiva and I leading the field home to land the Princess Royal Willmott Dixon Stakes run at Ascot, 1999.

Leo and I at a family show jumping event. I adore to watch the children ride and help with the ponies.

My one and only race with Rocco at Ascot, 2017. You can see from the grins on our faces just how much fun it was!

Very happy to win the Prix de
Diane Longines at Chantilly, 2015.

In the drive position, riding for Cheveley Park Stud at Ascot, 2017.

Embracing my father after winning a big race in Milan. It's always fantastic when he's able to come and watch me ride.

Celebrating another Royal Ascot win with Peter Phillips after riding Baitha Alga to victory in the 2014 Norfolk Stakes.

Winning at Sha Tin in Hong Kong, 2019. It's amazing to think I've been riding in Hong Kong for over 30 years. I never dreamed I'd have a career so international.

Winning the Breeders' Cup Turf on the great Enable, 2018.
She really was one of the true greats.

Giving Enable a grateful kiss after winning the Darley Irish Oaks in Kildare, 2017. I always gave her a kiss after a win!

Over the moon with my boys, Leo and Rocco. I love this picture of us celebrating in the weighing room on the July Course in Newmarket, where we often go as a family.

(From left to right) Lester, me, Her Majesty the Queen and Ian Balding. I had to pinch myself!

Receiving the trophy for the Longines World's Best Jockey, 2019.
It's truly incredible; I didn't expect my career to still be going at this point,
let alone winning this award for the last three years.

Celebrating winning the Prince of Wales's Stakes at Ascot with Rewilding, 2011. This is one of the most sought-after prizes at the Royal Meeting, as it always includes the best horses in the world in the race. For me it warranted a higher jump!

doing or anything like that. I tell the truth: I was tired, angry and frustrated, which is why I did it, but that decision was entirely on me. No one forced me. I fucked up, but I didn't kill anyone. I'm of good character, I always try to promote racing wherever I go and whatever I do.

They suspend me for six months, the minimum. It's backdated a few weeks to the initial announcement of my suspension. The ban will end on 19 May, which means I'll miss the 1000 and 2000 Guineas but will be free to ride the Derby in early June and at Royal Ascot a few weeks later.

If anyone will have me, that is.

We go to South Africa on safari, to Dubai, to Thailand and to Australia and New Zealand. We go to Uluru and the Gold Coast. I climb Sydney Harbour Bridge, which scares the crap out of me because I get really bad vertigo, and in New Zealand I go bungee jumping, which scares even more crap out of me. I'm like Mr Bean off the top of the diving board, terrified and shaking and wanting to get down. My kids think this is the funniest thing they've ever seen, funnier even than the farce of hiding me in the back of the car whenever we wanted to leave the house with all the paparazzi about.

At Universal Studios in LA, we do *The Simpsons* ride. Two years ago I freaked out and started screaming when they put the bar down: it triggered too many memories of being trapped in the plane at Newmarket. This time, I make it through OK. It just goes to show, I guess, that progress is never gradual, expected or even. My career might be at a crossroads, and who knows what'll happen when I return, but in one aspect of my life at least I'm still moving forwards.

For almost a month we have nothing but sunshine and relaxation, and then on New Year's Day we're back in England in the cold and grey. For the first time in almost two decades I won't be going back out to the sun to ride Godolphin's horses in the desert. I won't be riding any horses at all, come to think of it: certainly not competitively.

I'm just thinking that I can't let myself mope around the place for another four and a half months when Pete rings.

'Frankie,' he says, 'what's the one thing you said you'd never do?'

'You know the answer to that. Any of those bloody reality TV shows.'

'Yes, well. You're not getting paid at the moment, which means I'm not getting paid either. So I've booked you in for *Celebrity Big Brother*.'

'You've done *what*?'

'It starts on Thursday.'

'Pete, today's Tuesday.'

'I know. No time like the present, is there? Good luck.'

I don't know the first thing about *Big Brother*. I've watched it a couple of times, but without really paying too much attention. I thought it was just sitting in a room with 12 crazy people. I didn't know there were games, rules and tasks.

I don't take it that seriously. To get the full amount of money they've agreed, I have to last 25 days: that's it. I don't have to win, I just have to not get kicked out early. So I decide I'll just be myself, not get involved in any bullshit, and wait it out that way. Some people take it really seriously and are forever working out tactics. I can't be bothered with all that. Partly it's what different people want out of their stay in the *Big Brother* house, as that word 'celebrity' is a pretty loose one. There are those who aren't that well known and who are doing it because they want to raise their profile, and those who are only 'celebrities' by virtue of having been on reality shows. I don't need to raise my profile, and I'm well known through being damn good at my job. I'm doing this because I need the money: nothing more, nothing less. And I reckon I'm the most normal person in here. That's a first.

We have no contact with the outside world: no phones, computers, news, emails, nothing. We don't even have any clocks. I do lots of the cooking, as I really enjoy it, and I use the position of the sun overhead to work out roughly when I should serve lunch. Cooking, chopping, washing: that's my time, and I guard it preciously. I even take up smoking, purely because so many of the housemates pop outside for cigarette breaks and if I want to continue the conversation then I have to be out there with them or sitting on my own inside like Billy No-Mates.

I use the time to reflect, which I haven't really had the chance to do: the last few months have been such a whirl of leaving Godolphin, waiting for the drugs test result, dealing with the fallout, then jetting off with the family. Exactly a decade ago I was in a similar position: not being banned and leaving my job, of course, but forced to consider what I really wanted to do with my life. Back then I chose to go back to being a jockey rather than go down the rabbit hole of the celebrity circuit. Nothing I see in this house makes me want to do anything different this time. My ban ends in the third week of May, and I'll be champing at the bit to get back racing by then.

*   *   *

The moment I leave the *Big Brother* house, I start training again. I ride out at Coolmore once a week, I work on my Equicizer, I get myself fit. I'm going to hit the ground running.

News breaks that Mahmood has been caught doping some of his horses and been banned from racing for eight years. The BHA found banned steroids in samples taken from 11 horses, and Mahmood himself admitted doping four others. All Godolphin's hard work has been ruined by one person. When I say ruined, I mean he's given it a really, really bad reputation. And why, when you train 300 horses, do you need to do that?

What do I think? Gosh, so many things all at once. He was the one who wanted me out: he was the one who pretty much forced me out. And now it turns out he was doping horses and dragging Godolphin's name through the mud. Part of me is glad that he's got his comeuppance and been punished for what he's done. He never had the decency to give me an explanation for the way he behaved towards me, so don't ask me to feel sorry for him now when the wheel's turned and he's on the receiving end.

Another part of me thinks that if only I'd bitten the bullet and stuck it out for six more months at Godolphin, everything would have gone back to normal once the trainer who didn't like or rate me was gone and I was back with those who did. But I couldn't have known any of that at the time. And I'm certainly not going to go to Godolphin and ask for my old job back. For a start, they wouldn't give it to me and second, I wouldn't want it. As the old saying goes, you can never step in the same river twice, as you're not the same, and neither is the river.

I've only got a fortnight left to serve of my ban when I go to Newmarket to watch the 2000 Guineas. Sheikh Mohammed's there – his horse Dawn Approach is the favourite – and as I'm walking through the stands I see him having lunch.

It's now or never. I start walking towards him almost without realising it. Six months ago I spent a week in Dubai trying to see him and being fobbed off by all and sundry. I wanted to thank him for all that he'd done, and that hasn't changed. So this is my chance.

I walk right up to his table. He looks up and sees me.

'Sheikh Mohammed,' I say, 'thank you very much for everything you've done for me.'

For a moment his face is unreadable, then he smiles and gestures for a chair to be brought.

'Please,' he says, 'why don't you sit down for lunch?'

'That's kind, but I can't. I just wanted to say thank you. Those were 18 good years.'

'They were, weren't they? Thank you, Frankie.'

And that's it. As I walk away, I almost physically feel as though a weight has been lifted.

The ban's supposed to be lifted on 19 May, which means I could, at a push, think about getting a Derby mount two weeks later, but in the end I only start riding again on 31 May: 12 days lost because of seemingly endless bureaucratic glitches between France Galop and the BHA which delay the reissue of my jockey's licence. After six months out, another half a month, more or less, is incredibly frustrating, but I try to be Zen about it. *Play the long game, Frankie*, I tell myself.

I'm nervous about my comeback, and I'd be lying if I were to say that I'm not. But I'm more nervous about people's perception. I'm not too nervous about my riding because it's something I've done all my life. For the last nine months I've been in the news for the wrong reasons, so I don't know what people think of me now. I'd like to think it's going to be easy peasy, that I'll be welcomed back like the prodigal son. Good old Frankie, he's back. And now I'm a free agent, I'll have owners and trainers queuing up to book me for their best rides, won't I?

I wait for my phone to start ringing off the hook.
I wait, and I wait, and I wait.
Silence.

6

INSPIRED

Nobody phones. I can hardly beg a ride. People that I thought were my friends fob me off with lame excuses. I'm not flavour of the month, and maybe I should have expected that. It's another Catch-22: because I'm damaged goods then people won't want me until they see I can still win races for them, but they won't be able to see that unless they give me a chance to ride for them.

I realise that the break from Godolphin wasn't just a one-time thing, done and dusted last year. It has ripples which spread outwards, and the biggest ripple of all is how influential Godolphin are. An outfit that rich and powerful controls a lot of people, either directly or indirectly. There are trainers who aren't allowed to give me rides, and there are trainers who could give me rides but don't want to for fear that they'll get blowback from Godolphin. No one says this directly; no one needs to.

It's just a general unspoken threat. It's not even necessarily coming straight from Godolphin. But that's the influence they have.

So whereas before I could ride for almost anyone but Coolmore if Godolphin didn't need me, now that range of rides is halved. I'm basically starting from scratch again. I feel like a character in a Dick Francis novel, the washed-up ex-jockey who had it all and blew it.

Finally, I get three rides at Epsom. I'm supposed to go by helicopter, but it's foggy in Newmarket and we can't take off. I switch to Plan B, driving; but driving of course runs the risk helicopters don't, of being stuck in traffic, and that's what happens. I can't believe it: my first ride for six months, and I'm going to miss it.

The clock ticks on and on. The traffic inches forward. My stress levels are going through the roof: I can't remember the last time I was this nervous. After six months out, and then another fortnight because of bureaucracy, this would be just typical. And even when we reach the racecourse, the queues for the car parks are still miles long, and we can't get past. I look at my watch. I have to get to the weighing room now or lose the rides – the first ride, at least. Missing my comeback wouldn't be a great look. It's been hard enough getting the rides in the first place. The least I can do is turn up.

At the three-furlong marker I hop out of the car and run to the rail, where a couple of security guards stop me.

'Could I see your badge please, sir?' one says.

'I don't have a badge.'

'Then you have to go to the main entrance.'

'I'm a jockey and I'm about to miss my first race.'

'If you go to the main entrance, sir, they'll sort you out.'

I haven't got time to go to the main entrance, and I don't want to play the 'Do you know who I am?' card. Almost before I know it, I've ducked past them, jumped the rail and am running the last three furlongs. I don't look behind to see if they're chasing me, and I don't care if they are or not: I'm not going to miss this.

The rush actually takes my worries away. Helmet on, straight out: I don't have time to get nervous. My first ride is on Beatrice Aurore, who doesn't do brilliantly with the camber in Epsom's straight and fades away rather tamely to finish last. Then I'm on Fattsota, who finishes fifth behind Neil Callan and Resurge. Neil was due to be riding Sri Putra in the next, but the ride's been given to me, and Neil's understandably not happy about it – especially when Channel 4's Emma Spencer, obviously not knowing about the switch, asks him how he rates his chances on Sri Putra, a horse he's ridden in its previous 13 races. 'Let's not get into the politics of that,' Neil snaps. 'We'll enjoy the winner and talk about the rest later.' He also retweets a number of Twitter comments, including one which says about me: 'Wow, no loyalty, the bloke cheated and gets treated like a hero.'

After all the fuss, Sri Putra fades in the straight to finish last.

So my first three races back have yielded two last places and a fifth out of eight. Hardly the stuff of which fairy tales are made. And it's not just Neil who's pissed off: the other two rides also came at the expense of other jockeys who were originally booked but then replaced when I became available. As always when this kind of thing happens – and it does happen, more often than people like to think – the one person not to blame is the incoming jockey. These decisions are made by owners and trainers, and no jockey in his right mind is going to turn down the chance of a good ride: it's a freelance business, and everyone takes what they can get. Like every jockey, I've been on both sides of the equation, and of course one's much nicer than the other, but the important thing to remember is that it's never personal.

I've missed the buzz of the racing and am pleased to be back. I'm surprised how well I've done today with my fitness, even if I've still got a bit of a J.Lo bum which I need to shed. The reality is setting in: this is a new challenge in every way, and I'm a little bit afraid of the future. I know that's natural, but it's still a weird feeling. I remind myself to stay positive and keep a good clear head.

My first dozen races back are all winless. I'm hoping that Sandown will change this. Looking at the form, I figure I've got three live chances. The first one, Blurred Vision, is inexperienced and has a poor outside draw, so she misses the break when it goes. Next up is Asian Trader, and she too misses the first kick, but I feel she's got more to give and so I don't panic. There's not much time or distance left – it's only five furlongs, over in less than a minute – but I wait for the gap to open up in front of me. When you've got a horse that can travel, you can always find some room at Sandown, and I do. I urge Asian Trader through, and that's it: we cross the line in front, and the monkey is thrown off my back at the dozenth time of asking.

I do the flying dismount off Asian Trader. In normal times I wouldn't bother, not for a race this small, an ordinary sprint handicap on an evening card at Sandown, but beggars can't be choosers. This is my first win back. It means a whole lot more than it would normally do. There are probably 100 punters gathered around the enclosure, and they seem to appreciate it.

Although I've logged the first winner of my new career, the hard work has only really just begun. I realise that the idea that I'd just pick up where I left off was ludicrous. Six months is by far the longest I've been out of racing for since I began my career almost 25 years ago. Even after the plane crash in 2000 I was only out for a little more than two months. I've been training and riding out, so I haven't forgotten how to sit on a horse or ride one, but there's a world of difference between galloping solo or in tandem on Newmarket Heath and running with a dozen other horses in a race. I'm back to where I was in 2003, when I'm trying too hard to make things happen. My arms are doing what my brain's telling them not to do, and in traffic as often as not I'll lose ground by pulling the horse wide to go for the safer route. The more mistakes I make the more I lose confidence, which makes me ride even worse, and the vicious circle goes on.

It's not that there are fewer good rides than before, it's that far more of those good rides are sewn up by stables and retained jockeys. The halcyon days of the traditional owner-breeder have gone. I used to have a steady supply of impeccably bred colts and fillies. No longer. I'm going to be just another jobbing jockey on the lookout for a good ride. Problem is, there are lots of those kind of guys, and most of them are much younger than me. But are they hungrier?

At one stage I go 50 races without a winner. Fifty! Even by the law of averages, you'd probably be bound to have at least one or two in that time simply by sitting on the horse and pointing it in the right direction. Again the vicious circle: I'm struggling to get winners, which means trainers become more reluctant to give me decent horses, which means that I'm less likely to ride winners, and so on.

I can't see anything coming up. I didn't expect it would be so hard to fit back in. I'm going to give it till the end of the season, and if nothing's come up by then, I'll pack it in. Oh, they'll say I gave up, I couldn't hack it, Godolphin were right after all, and so on. I don't care. Let them say what they say. Everyone has to retire sometime: not everyone always gets what they want. I've got lots of options, inside and outside racing. I'll be OK.

Catherine sits me down. 'You keep telling us how fucking good you are. Well, now would be a good time to show it.'

*   *   *

At Royal Ascot, a representative of Qatar's Sheikh Joaan al Thani approaches me. We'd like to offer you a job, he says. Stable jockey for Al Shaqab Racing.

I ask how many horses they have.

About 50 in England and 80 in France. He's focusing on quality rather than quantity, so I won't have vast numbers of horses to ride and will have a lot of time to ride for other people. But there are some very good prospects among those horses: Style Vendome, who's just won the Poule d'Essai des Poulains (the French equivalent of the 2000 Guineas); Toronado, second in the St James's Palace Stakes; and Olympic Glory, a Group 1 winner. He's got plans to expand, so it's something that suits us both: a good opportunity for me to get back in the big league, and for him to be able to use an experienced jockey. His colours are nicely understated, grey with red epaulettes – not as instantly visible as Godolphin's royal blue, but that doesn't matter.

I ask Dad what he thinks.

'A job is better than no job,' he replies. 'Take it.'

I go to meet Sheikh Joaan at Chantilly. I find myself on the same train as the racing journalists, who know that I'm not riding, so of course they're keen to find out what I'm doing here. Just fancied a day at the races, I say.

I meet Sheikh Joaan's racing manager, Harry Herbert. He's Lord Porchester's son – racing's a small world. I sit in their box for three hours until every race is finished. No sign of Sheik Joaan. These things happen, and I know by now in my career not to get stressed by them. I leave the box, and am just walking towards the main gates when I get a text telling me that Sheikh Joaan's arrived after all.

I run back upstairs and find him in deep conversation with Criquette Head-Maarek. Criquette's one of France's top trainers, and a couple of hours ago her filly Treve won the Prix de Diane, France's equivalent of the Oaks. Sheikh Joaan wants to buy Treve.

'I'm so pleased you've got Frankie,' she says. 'He'll be a great match for Treve.'

I ride Treve at morning work, and she's an aeroplane, up there with the best fillies I've ever ridden. From the moment I get on her, I know she's a superstar. Some horses you can just feel it, and she's one of those. She's not that big, but boy, when she goes, she goes. Her acceleration is dazzling.

I'm riding Treve in the Prix Vermeille, three weeks before the Arc. It's a strong field, but even so Criquette and I decide that we should do not much more than the bare minimum: hold her in the pack for as long as possible and then let her change of gear do the rest.

I keep her on the rail and near the back until the final stages, and then with two furlongs left I ease her out between two runners and ask her to go. She just flies. Wild Coco's out in front, but we go past her like she's standing still and win by a couple of lengths going away.

'She didn't do anything today,' Criquette tells the press. 'She's hardly breathing and she only raced for a furlong as she was held in. She was a bit fresh today, so we should have some more to come in the Arc.'

To be riding a horse like this so soon after my comeback is more than I could reasonably have hoped for. It's my first Group 1 success since returning. I'm back in the limelight, I've got a great horse. *Phew!* I think. *There is a God, and He's given me another chance.*

Treve's installed as second favourite for the Arc, but I reckon she's as good as any horse in that field. I've won the Arc three times, but I'd trade them all for a victory here and what it would mean: that I'm back beyond any reasonable doubt, and I'm here to stay for a while yet.

There's a meeting at Nottingham on the Wednesday, three days before the Arc, and I take a couple of rides just to keep my eye in. I ride Fair Flutter to victory in the opening race, but as we're going to the stalls for the next one, Eland Ally rears up and unseats me. I land hard on my foot, and instantly a searing pain shoots up my ankle. Please God, let it be just a twist or a sprain. Anything which I can strap up, pop the painkillers and still ride the Arc.

I can't put any weight on my right ankle as I try to stand up. The course doctor tells me it's a sprain, just soft tissue with no bone damage. But I know the difference: the pain from a broken bone is somehow deeper and hotter than simple ligament damage. *No*, I say, it's a break, I know it is, so I need an X-ray.

They give me one in Cambridge. Broken in three places, including the only bone in the foot where the blood can't get to. It gives me no pleasure to be right. That's it. Arc gone, Breeders' Cup gone, Melbourne Cup gone, the rest of the season gone.

Thierry Jarnet, who rode Treve to victory in the Prix de Diane, gets the ride.

'It's bad luck for Frankie,' Criquette says, 'but that's life in racing.'

Dr Robinson operates on Saturday, making sure to place the screws so they won't stop me riding. Jockeys need a lot of movement in the feet and lower leg to ride: our ankles are shock absorbers, basically. Dr Robinson does all the jockeys, so he knows exactly what we need to do our jobs.

The hospital keep me in overnight, and on Sunday morning they send me home in a cast and with painkillers. I ring my neighbour, Tim Gredley.

'Mate, come round and watch the Arc with me.'

I have a strange half-and-half feeling. I want Treve to win, because it would be good for Sheikh Joaan and I'll be riding her in future, but also I don't want her to win because that should be me up there. The field is one of the strongest I can remember, but she makes it look easy. It's like watching a Rolls-Royce. Thierry runs her wide at the back, and I think he might have screwed this up, but then he turns on the turbos and Treve streaks to victory. Thierry's ridden her well, but to be honest the form she's in Thierry Henry could have ridden her to victory.

That would have been my 200th Group 1 winner, my fourth Arc, and me back on the big stage again. That should have been me, could have been me, would have been me. Should have, could have, would have: last words of a fool.

'Tim,' I say.

'Yes?'

'Do me a favour and go home, please.'

The moment he shuts the door behind him, I burst into tears, and I don't stop all afternoon. The painkillers

I take later that day aren't for my ankle: they're for my broken heart. It's like my life is a giant snakes and ladders board. These last few months I've been climbing that ladder, slowly and with great effort – and now I've gone sliding all the way back down to the ground again.

I try to put everything into perspective. I'm not dead, I'm still going to come back, and the filly is still going to be there for me. It's just bad luck. Just bad luck.

I finish 2013 with 16 winners, and 2014 isn't much better, only yielding 37 winners. More than double last year's, but that's not saying much, especially when you consider that in 2013 I basically only had half a season once injuries and time served during the ban are taken into account.

My big hope for 2014 is Treve, ranked the best horse in the world last year. I ride her twice: in the Prix Ganay at Longchamp and the Prince of Wales at Royal Ascot. At Longchamp, we lose out to Cirrus des Aigles by a short neck, one of those races that could have gone either way: Cirrus des Aigles is a multiple Group winner and a very good horse, so a narrow defeat isn't a surprise and certainly isn't a disgrace.

Ascot's different. Treve has sore feet, and there's been so little rain that the track's like a road. She's odds-on, but I can tell even as we canter up to the start that something's wrong. I get her up to second in the straight but that's the limit of it, and we end up third.

I'm blamed for it, but it wasn't my fault. I know when I've lost races off my own bat, and I always hold my hands up to it. But no jockey in the world would have got a better result than me. And she's still favourite for the Arc. Twelve months after I should have ridden her in it, this will be my moment, I'm sure of it.

Sheikh Joaan wants to see me. I'm flown to Mykonos and taken to his family's yacht.

'Criquette doesn't want you on Treve,' he says. 'She thinks you don't suit the filly. Thierry will ride her in the Prix Vermeille and the Arc.'

Criquette points to the fact that Treve has run twice this season, both odds-on and both ridden by me, and lost each time, whereas Thierry won the Arc and the Prix de Diane on her. But there were reasons for both those defeats, and I've been riding well: it's only a fortnight since I won two Group 1s on the same day in France.

'There's no reason against Frankie,' Criquette tells the media. 'He's a great jockey. It's more the filly than anything else.'

Someone asks her if Treve would have won her two races this year if Thierry had ridden her rather than me. She pauses before replying: 'No, I wouldn't say that.'

It tears the heart out of me. Last year was just blind chance and bad luck, which happens to every jockey. This is different, and though of course I accept that Sheikh Joaan and Criquette only want the best for Treve and the stables as a whole, that doesn't mean I have to like it. It brings back memories of two years ago and Encke in the St Leger, and those aren't memories I need or want rekindled.

And even in that case, I was being pushed aside for younger riders who Godolphin saw as the future and part of their forward planning. Here, Thierry's three years older than I am, and most of his big wins were in years which began with '19' rather than '20'. He's almost the anti-me: no flying dismounts or extravagant celebrations, no media profile, and certainly no drugs busts. He's quiet, introverted, private, and whereas I love my food he's supposed to have a diet which even by jockey standards is pretty spartan.

When I'm asked about it, I'm terse and don't try and joke it away. 'I have nothing to say on the matter, but I am very disappointed and that's it.' One sentence, that's all I give: because otherwise I'd talk their hind legs off and it wouldn't be helpful for me, Sheikh Joaan, Criquette or Thierry.

Thierry probably can't believe his luck. 'I believed I wouldn't ride the filly again when she was bought by

Sheikh Joaan, because he had a contract with another jockey and that's the reality of racing at the moment,' he says. 'You know that one day you have the ride and the next you don't. You have to remain calm about it. Lanfranco is professional enough to know it happens and to bounce back. I know her by heart and have been around her since her debut. Maybe there is a bit more feeling that passes between horse and rider. The circumstances in which Lanfranco took over were a little unlucky. Obviously there was a lot of pressure because she had won the Arc and was still unbeaten. There are a lot of different things that can happen in a race. But she remains a filly with a lot of quality and you have to try and extract the best from her. In the Arc, I tried to ride just the filly and not ride a race. Perhaps that made the difference.'

I'm still Sheikh Joaan's retained rider, and it's made clear that this is absolutely a one-off scenario. Harry says: 'It's Criquette's choice and she knows it's been a painful one for Frankie. But she feels Thierry knows the filly so well and rides her in her work. He is around her a lot and these last two races are so critical, especially the Arc itself, that she requested Thierry ride the filly. She just feels the two of them get on and know one another so well. These small percentages are critical for these big races, especially when you only have two more bullets to fire and very big bullets they are, too.

'Frankie's been amazing. He's a remarkable team player. He's very disappointed but at the same time he knows there's a lot of very nice horses out there that he'll still be riding for the Sheikh. This is in no way a reflection of what anyone thinks of Frankie. There's been no falling-out, it's just one of those wretched things. He's loving the job, he's ridden some fantastic races, like when he won the Prix Morny the other day. I think this job is really suiting him and he looks in great shape.'

I still get an Arc ride: Ruler of the World, last year's Derby winner, for Coolmore. Last year Thierry rode Treve round the outside. This year he hugs the rail, and right from the start I can see how well Treve's going: the way she travels, the way she quickens when Thierry asks her to. It's so amazing, seeing a superlative horse at the top of her game. This is the Treve of old, not the one I rode at Ascot. God, what would I give to be on her now?

Ruler of the World and I finish ninth. It's not any better watching what should have been your horse win from five lengths back than it was from my sofa with a cast on my ankle. That's two Arcs which should have been mine and aren't.

* * *

Leo's supposed to be playing polo at Cowdray Park, but it's absolutely hammering it down. We spend the night talking and drinking with some of the other parents, and though they're all hopeful that the rain will ease and the kids will get to play the next day, I'm not so optimistic. Sure enough, the next day the field's so waterlogged that the only game they could possibly play there is water polo.

We get in the lorry and set off home. We've got a fair schlepp ahead of us, about three hours. Catherine's at the wheel, and I say I fancy a glass of wine, so we stop at the nearest garage. I get some shitty Pinot Grigio in a screw-top bottle and a few nibbles. Back on the road, I pour myself a glass and put my feet up on the dashboard. I get a text from my mate Rab Havlin, who's second-string jockey to William Buick at Clarehaven, John Gosden's stables.

William's gone to Godolphin, it says.

I almost drop my Pinot Grigio. John's one of the best trainers, and best men, in racing, and Prince Khalid Abdullah of Saudi Arabia supplies him with some great horses. So for William to up sticks and go to Godolphin – well, there must be some serious money involved to prise him away. Although being one of their retained riders is about the most prestigious position a jockey can have in world racing, Godolphin have actually had a pretty mediocre season by their standards, and I've heard rumours that they're going to make Mickaël concentrate more on their French horses and ditch Silvestre altogether. But rumours fly the whole time, and nine times out of 10 they turn out to be a load of rubbish. Not this time, clearly.

I read the text to Catherine and say, with a laugh, 'Should I text John and see if he'll have me back?' Ha ha, funny joke. I'm not being remotely serious.

She's about to answer when my phone rings again.

JOHN G, the display says. Talk about timing.

'Hey, boss. I've just got a text from Rab.'

'I thought you might have. Listen, matey, I've got a plan.'

'Yes?'

'I'm not going to get anyone in for the rest of the season, there's no point, and William's going to ride out his contract anyway. So here's my thinking. Don't breathe a word of this to anyone, but do what you have to do, do all your stuff in the Middle East over the winter with Sheikh Joaan, I don't want to step on his toes either now or next season – and basically, I'll see you at Clarehaven on 1 March, ready to go.'

The old gang, back together again. I hang up, drain my glass and yell my head off like a kid with a sugar rush on Christmas Day.

*　　*　　*

And on 1 March 2015 that's just where I am: at Clarchaven, ready to go. John hasn't told anyone I'm coming back, and the warmth of the welcome when I do really touches me. His lads are a real mix of nationalities, a mini-UN – Pakistanis, Indians, Brazilians, French, Czech, Spanish – and every one of them hugs me and seems pleased for me. All my old pals I remember from 20 years back are still there. It's just the same, but it's also different, because first time round I was more or less a kid and now I'm a grown man. It's an old cliché, but like the best clichés it's only so because it's true: it really does feel like coming home. I've been so excited about this all winter, and it's everything I thought it would be.

It's strange. I always thought that it would be the wins which would matter most, but in actual fact some of the most intense moments of happiness I've known have been when I've been saved.

'Here,' John says, 'let's start you on this guy. He's all over the place, but by God he's got some raw ability.'

'What's his name?'

'Golden Horn.'

John's right, both about Golden Horn's ability and his waywardness. I come off our first work ride with a big smile on my face.

'What do you think?' he asks.

'John, this horse is good but I need to teach him a lot more. He feels very mature but a bit of a dope. I wouldn't mind riding him again, that's for sure.'

There's another really good three-year-old in John's stable, Jack Hobbs. He's mightily impressive, a brilliant workhorse; he's exuberant whereas Golden Horn will just do enough in training. I ride Jack Hobbs at York in the Dante Stakes, a major trial race for the Derby, with William on Golden Horn. We were thinking of the Guineas for Golden Horn but I didn't think he's mature enough to keep the speed for a mile.

We're 2/1 favourites, but in the last furlong we've got no match for Golden Horn's pace and finish almost three lengths adrift. The difference between the two horses is clear. Jack Hobbs is very good, but he's also a big baby when compared with Golden Horn.

I really, really, really want to ride Golden Horn in the Derby, but William has a good rapport with him, and unless Godolphin enter a runner he'll probably get the nod.

Ella and I do a pairs showjumping competition together. We win, and I'm as made up for her as I am for myself in any of the big races: a real proud dad moment. We stay for the prizegiving, and when they say 'the winners are Ella and Frankie Dettori' all the tiger mums go mad. 'That's not allowed!' they cry. 'He's a professional jockey!'

I'm having none of it. 'Listen, I'm riding with my daughter. I won a rosette!'

I know exactly how hard I need to work every morning and for how long to lose 3lb, and I know that when I do, I'll feel better: alert and aggressive. Less than 3lb and I don't feel the benefits; more than 3lb and I start to have ill effects. Three pounds is the sweet spot, my Goldilocks number.

Sheikh Mohammed's seen something he likes in Jack Hobbs, and buys a half share in him. That means William will ride him in the Derby, and I get to ride Golden Horn.

I've been praying for this opportunity ever since I came back, the chance to ride a superstar horse. I thought I had it with Treve, but that didn't turn out quite how I'd hoped. *Please God*, I ask, *let this one work out better. I've had some real lows these past years, some of my own doing, some not. Please let this be one of those times when the rollercoaster's on the way up rather than hurtling downwards.*

A second really good shot at the Derby, eight years

after I won it and two years since my comeback. Of all the races I've ever ridden, two stand out above the others, the Derby and the Arc, and until and unless I win one of them I won't regard my comeback as a success. I should have had two more Arc winners by now. Maybe third time's the charm.

And now here we are, at Epsom on Derby Day, with the big race just around the corner. There's one last piece of preparation I need: the lucky white tape. Before the 2007 race, knowing how desperate I was to win, one of the sound engineers called Pete Binfield said, 'You need some of my lucky white tape, Frankie.' It was a tradition which dated back to 1989, when he patched up a tear in Willie Carson's saddle before Willie went out and won the Derby on Nashwan. In 2007, he put a wrap of tape around my right stirrup, and I won on Authorized.

So now we do the same thing again, a wrap around my right stirrup, and see if it'll work the oracle once more.

I used to run from fear. Now I embrace it. Epsom at its finest, the crowds expectant, the horses in the stall. Here we go.

Golden Horn wants to go out too fast and have his own way. No, I say, come here. I'm in charge, not you.

While Elm Park and Hans Holbein fight it out at the front, I settle Golden Horn at the back and put him to sleep, using every ounce of my experience to switch the telegraph in his brain from 'full steam ahead' to 'cruise'. I have to be strong enough to control him but sympathetic enough to make him still want to run, and that's something I can do instinctively by now, keeping him on the cusp between the two like finding the biting point on a clutch.

I've got so much experience that it's like playing chess. I can see two moves ahead: I see the race not as it is right now, but as it will be in a few seconds' time. I know that one horse in front of me will go left and the other will go right. I don't even know how I know this: it's little tells I'm not even conscious of, tiny pieces of memory stored in my brain which come up just when I need them. I've seen every move there is out there: there's nothing on a racecourse which could surprise me. When I'm out there and in the zone then everything else just fades away. It's not even that I'm in the race: I *am* the race.

All the way up the hill, round the corner and down the slope, I hang back. As we turn for home in the final straight Hans Holbein is clear off the front and I'm ninth of 12. I can see William's familiar royal blue colours on Jack Hobbs in front of me, and I know he's the man I have to beat. *Track Jack Hobbs all the way and then go two furlongs out.*

I swing Golden Horn to the outside with three to go and start to make up ground on the others. There's no feeling in racing better than this, coming from a long way back on a powerful horse and picking off my rivals one by one. Epicuris, Storm the Stars and Giovanni Canaletto all seem to be going backwards as we fly past them.

Jack Hobbs is still ahead of me, right where I want him. Always better to be the hunter than the hunted in these situations. He's out in front, but I'm closing the gap. I go after him. For a moment or so I hit a flat spot, Golden Horn's relentless acceleration seeming to splutter like a car misfire, but almost before I have the time to urge him on again he's back on it, eating up the turf.

We flash past the furlong marker. It's me and Jack Hobbs, with the rest scrapping it out for third. For a moment we're neck and neck, running stride for stride: but Jack Hobbs is tightening and tying up while Golden Horn is still running like a champ, and I know we're going to win. One hundred and fifty metres to go and this is all sewn up.

It's as though someone's just pulled the plug. I'm suddenly zapped of all energy, and my body feels like jelly. I have no strength, none at all. I feel like I'm going to be sick. It's the most extraordinary thing. Intense.

Immense. All the tension, the hopes, the fears, the stress, the fall which took me off Treve two years ago and Criquette taking the ride from me last year, everything I've been through these past few years: all of that is just sucked clean out of me, and for a few seconds I'm an empty vessel clinging onto a magnificent horse. All those years of darkness, and now the sun has come out.

I snap back into myself with a few strides left and am punching the air even before we cross the line. I can't get to the bottom of this horse, and I can hardly pull him up at the end of the race: he feels like he'd go round and do it all over again.

In all my years of riding, in all the races I've won, it's the best and most exciting moment. More than the seven, more than my first Derby, more than anything. They told me I was finished. They told me I'd never be the same jockey again. They told me I should head off into the sunset and let the young bucks fight it out.

They were wrong. They were all wrong. Frankie Dettori, two-time Derby winner. How do you like them apples? I look down at my breeches. L. Dettori, they say. L for Lanfranco. And now L for Lazarus.

I see John. He's not really the high-fiving type, but the look of deep satisfaction on his face thrills me as much as anything I'm feeling. Eighteen years ago I was due to ride Benny the Dip for him here, but Godolphin entered

Bold Demand at the last minute, I had to ride that instead, and Willie Ryan won on Benny the Dip. That's almost two decades I've waited for the chance to win the Derby with John, the man who twice now has given me a chance and believed in me when few others did. Back then he was very much a father figure to me when I was young and wayward. Now we're much more old mates, or at a push he's like a big brother.

We've done it, and it's indescribably special, as is he. I see the way he is not just with his horses but his staff too. There's an old Latin phrase, *oderint dum metuant*, attributed to the Emperor Caligula: 'let them hate, so long as they fear'. Some trainers run their stables like that. Not John. He listens to everyone's opinion, treats everyone equally, takes his own time to train people to do their jobs properly, and wins their respect 100 per cent. He's a great human being. People love him, but few of them more than I do.

I work better and more instinctively with him than I have with any other trainer. We read from the same sheet. He trains horses to suit my riding, I ride horses to suit his training. I don't even know exactly how the chemistry works, just that it's there. Sometimes we don't even need to talk to each other to understand what the other's thinking. It just works. It's not one big thing, it's a hundred little things which all add up. He knows how to get the best out of me. If this was a football team and he was the manager, he wouldn't get me to run around the midfield for 90 minutes – he'd put me on up front with 15 minutes to go and say, 'Right, win this thing for us.' He knows when to give me a kick up the arse and when to put his arm round my shoulder, so every time I go out to ride for him I'm in the best place, mentally, that I can be. Sometimes I feel he knows me better than I know myself. When people use the word 'trainer', they mean someone who trains horses, but John trains me too, half the time.

'In the midst of winter,' Albert Camus once said in his essay, 'Return to Tipasa', 'I found there was, within me, an invincible summer.' I've known long winters these past few years, but for this summer, Golden Horn and I are all but invincible.

First we win the Eclipse, which has people talking about maybe even a run for the Arc, but as ever, John won't be rushed: 'A day at a time, a week at the time, the horse'll tell me. I watch, I listen, that's my job. It's up to the horse.' And that horse is progressing right before my eyes: filling out, becoming tougher, harder, more streetwise.

Then, after a blip on soft ground at the International Stakes when we lose to Arabian Queen by a neck, we win the Irish Champion Stakes at Leopardstown, though not before Golden Horn swerves suddenly to the right during the run-in and impedes Free Eagle. The stewards examine the footage and decide that he must have been spooked by the shadow of the grandstand on the course; certainly it was nothing I did, and indeed there was nothing I could have done to stop him, he jinked so quickly and suddenly.

Then we do take Golden Horn to the Arc, where Treve is going for a hat-trick of wins, something no horse has ever done before. She's won all three of her races this year, each one with Thierry riding her, and she's odds-on favourite to win this one too.

Sometimes it's a strange feeling, riding against a horse for whose stables you're the retained rider, but Criquette's made it so clear that she sees Thierry as Treve's jockey that I don't really think of it that way here. Do I want to beat her fair and square in a head-to-head? Of course. But more than that, much more than that, I want to win for Golden Horn, for John and for myself. A Derby–Arc double isn't unknown – six horses have done it in the last 50 years – but it is rare, and you need a special horse to pull it off.

Golden Horn is one of those horses.

Longchamp can be very tricky. We know he stays and we know he's good, and since we've got a difficult wide draw, I decide to use that rather than fight against it. I stay wide, well away from the other 17 runners and running on my own for the first two furlongs before slotting in behind the leader, Shahah. From the stands it may look bizarre, but I know what I'm doing: use a bit of energy to get the right spot, then settle back and cruise in Shahah's slipstream. In the Derby I bided my time and struck late, but he was playing up that day and I needed to put him to sleep before I could ask him to give me the full Golden Horn burst. Here he's right up for it, so I'm in the perfect position: on the leader's shoulder, close enough to the rail only to need to look over one shoulder rather than both for a move from behind, but not so close that I might get boxed in. That's how we run as we approach the home straight, with Flintshire on my outside hind flank in third.

Three furlongs to go and it's bubbling nicely; but in the Arc they come at your back with arrows, so I have to be careful not to let anyone get first run on me. Two furlongs to go and there are five or six horses abreast, but I have half a length jump on them. Once more I ask Golden Horn for his own special turbocharged kick, and once more he serves it up to me on a plate. His turn of foot just blows me away. I don't think even Dubai Millennium went this fast when I pushed the button. There's no horse in the world that can pass me now. From a furlong out

I'm just enjoying myself. With 75 metres left, I look back over my shoulder and see the sight every jockey loves: a world-class field swaying and struggling in my wake as Golden Horn powers on. What a horse. What a race. If the Derby win was my most emotional, this may well be my most assured. We've been in total control from start to finish, and he's put to bed a great Arc with great horses behind him like a real champion.

Treve is fourth. I'm sorry that she couldn't do the hat-trick, but there's a reason it's never been done, and that's because it's so hard to maintain that kind of form over three years. She's been a great mare, and Sheikh Joaan gives me a high five in the winner's enclosure, which is very sporting of him.

An Arc and a Derby in the same year. That's special.

'I think from Frankie's point of view, to him now at his age, he's not a kid any more,' John says. 'And these great victories, Arcs and Derbys, they mean everything to him now, where before there was going to be another one next year. We've known each other for many years and know each other very well, so that always helps and the unspoken word is usually more telling than the spoken word. I don't think we resurrected anything. All the ability, all the finesse, all the knowledge, it was all there. It was just that you need good horses to ride. I've always said, you don't put a driver in a Formula Two car and tell him to compete in a Formula One race. You'll get lapped. I never questioned him at all. It was a lack of opportunities that was his problem. Frankie is as good as ever, he really is, and he's still as hungry as ever, but I think the thing is that he's probably enjoying it more than he ever did, which I think is important.'

I am, and it is. It's everything.

Because Golden Horn's in such excellent condition – as John says, 'He's got such a constitution, you can hardly see a rib which is not usually the case at the end of a long campaign' – we decide to enter him in the Breeders' Cup. No horse has ever won the Arc and the Breeders' Cup in the same year, let alone a Derby–Arc–Breeders treble. If we could pull it off, that really would be an *annus mirabilis*. We're odds-on, but once more soft ground (there've been three inches of rain recently) does for us as it did at York, and the only other European runner, Found, beats us by half a length. It's frustrating to be on a horse so powerful but forced by the conditions to spin his wheels, but that's racing.

Two weeks later, Golden Horn is retired to stud at Dalham Hall. What a horse, and what a privilege to have ridden him this year.

'I'll never ride a better horse than that,' I tell John.

But, not for the first time, I'm plumb wrong.

7
ENABLE

In August 2016, I notch my 3,000th winner in front of 20,000 people. The fact that Jess Glynne's playing a gig after the racing finishes is pure coincidence when it comes to the crowd size, of course.

I start the night on 2,998 winners and only have three rides available to reach the mark. My first race is a victory on Ghayyar, and everyone thinks I'll make it in the next race on Blue Geranium, the only favourite I'm on tonight – but with two furlongs to go he weakens and ends up sixth, almost 30 lengths behind.

So now it's all down to Predilection, one of John's horses. John and I did the Derby–Arc double last year; how fitting would it be if my 3,000th came on one of his horses?

We're first out of the stalls and take up the running: if this is going to be a landmark, how better to do it than have 'made all' written against us in the notes to signify a horse which leads from stalls to tape? It's a mile race, and for six of those eight furlongs I set a steady pace. With two to go I urge Predilection to quicken, and inside the last I'm shaking him up to give me all he's got. He's hanging left and I have to keep him going straight, while Palmerston is closing on us, but the line's going to come for us before Palmerston does. The crowd are roaring long before I've even won, and I raise my arm to them as we finish clear. Three thousand! Not bad for someone who's only chased high numbers for four or five seasons at most.

Derek Thompson interviews me afterwards. 'I'm so proud of everyone for the support,' I say, 'and it's a beautiful touch to do it at Newmarket. I've got no more words.' That bit's not quite true; it rarely is, with me. 'I purposely didn't ride all week because I wanted to do it at Newmarket. This is where I'm from. I came here 30 years ago with a dream. Whoever thought I was going to ride 3,000 winners? All my friends are here. It's not a big meeting, it's not Royal Ascot, it's a mundane Friday night with 20,000 people. All my kids are here, I'm emotional. It was fabulous, I couldn't have written it better myself. I'm sixth in the all-time English standings. Doug Smith [3,112] is a realistic target and if I can be fifth all-time in the 350 years of English racing, it'd be a tremendous achievement for a young fella from Italy.'

John has a few words too. 'Just amazing! Frankie really has a sense of fulfilment, he's riding like a young man again, and 99 per cent of the time he behaves himself. But would you mind making sure he doesn't get on stage with Jess? I don't think she wants him up there.'

Like I said: he knows me better than I know myself sometimes.

The 20th anniversary of the Magnificent Seven comes round. Ladbrokes PR director Mike Dillon says there was 'weeping and teeth-gnashing' when the firm worked out it had lost £10 million, but adds: 'I remember at the time thinking it would be really good for racing [and betting on racing]. I told them: "Don't put that in the trading budget, put it in the marketing budget." It was the chance of a lifetime and the right guy to win those seven races. Had it been Lester "Stoneface" Piggott who did it, he'd have gone straight into the weighing room, no interviews, maybe smoked a cigar and that would be it. Frankie was brilliant, presented the cheque to every big winner, went on breakfast TV and every news channel known to man.'

I'm really glad Mike thinks that way, because that was exactly how I saw it – and still do. I take my job seriously, but I'm also here to entertain and to get as many people going to race meetings and watching on TV as possible. I love doing it: it's my way of giving something back to a sport which has given me so much.

Walter dies suddenly, aged only 55: an accidental fall from a bathroom window. It's such a shock that it takes me a while to fully accept it. He was one of the best riders I ever saw, maybe the most naturally talented of us all: a beautiful horseman with fantastically soft hands and an amazing ability to switch onto his horse's mood. He had a magic touch, and you can't teach someone that: either they have it or they don't. He did, and in spades.

Like a lot of jockeys, he found it hard to adjust to life after hanging up his boots. He had some success as a trainer – 270 winners in seven years – but I don't think it ever really filled the gap.

One of the stories I like most – and this was very Walter – was about the time he took his young daughters to a riding school in Hyde Park. Walter rode alongside them, and the instructor started telling him all the things that were wrong with his posture, his seat, the way he held the reins, and other things. Walter never let on who he was, but I can just imagine the enigmatic smile playing around his lips as the instructor went on and on.

*   *   *

Dad still rings me with advice whether I want it or not: you should have done this, you should have done that. That's the way he'll always be. Some things you can't change, so now I take no notice of it, but it took me long enough to get there.

The first part of my career, I was doing it for him because it was all about him. I was like a dog chasing my tail. I didn't know where I was going, I didn't know if I was happy or sad. I was just doing it to try to please him, and he was never happy. I wasn't having any fun. I was tortured inside. There was never enough. If I won five, he'd say I should have won six. If I won six, he'd say I should have won seven. Even when I won all seven he could probably have found something to be unhappy about.

And of course when you can never make someone happy, you're always trying to do exactly that: you always think that if you just do that little bit more then it will all come good. Until the day you realise that not only will it never happen, but also that it can never happen. You can never totally please someone who'll always find fault. And when I realised that, it all made sense, and I almost began to enjoy it. I started just to not bother engaging. I realised his game and how he was playing with my mind. I don't think he meant to do it half the time, but still: you get those patterns of behaviour which are so entrenched over many years, and someone has to break out of them or else they just go deeper and deeper.

We used to have the same old argument, again and again and again.

'Dad, what if I hadn't made it as a jockey? What if I'd failed?'

'You didn't fail. You're a champion. I did what I had to do to help you make it.'

'But what if it hadn't worked?'

'It did work.'

'Don't you see what a hard thing this is to do to a child? To send him away and brainwash him all the time that he has to make it to the top, because if he doesn't make it then his whole life will be ruined?'

'Frankie, it worked. I knew it would. I saw something in you that you didn't. That's why I did it.'

And of course there was never any resolution to this argument – you can only ever judge the life you've led rather than all the ones you haven't – but it took me years to be at peace with it. Sometimes you just have to agree to disagree. His thinking on some things is completely different to my thinking. Maybe that's partly from his upbringing, the way his parents came out from the war in poverty. Maybe it's a generational thing and it gets repeated *ad infinitum*; sometimes I have to bite my lip even if I think he's wrong, but I guess my kids probably think the same about me. And when they have kids of their own, they'll raise those kids very differently to how Catherine and I have raised them. It's the way things are.

I know Dad's got my back and has my best interests at heart, even – especially – if he's my worst critic. As a jockey, there's no one else I trust more to tell me whether I did something right or wrong. He can see things that slipped my mind, and sometimes even if I have my own plan it's nice to be reassured that I'm on the right lines.

Most of all, I know my dad loves me and he knows I love him, and that's all that really matters. That was his way of loving me, by pushing me to the extreme. He's a very strong character, my dad, much stronger than me. He did what he thought was right. I show my kids I love them in different ways. But the love is there regardless: it's just the way it comes out sometimes.

My 2017 season at Clarehaven starts with riding out on two fillies, Shutter Speed and Enable. Shutter Speed's a great worker, a flying machine in the morning: we go bombing along the gallops, and her appetite for work is incredible.

Enable, on the other hand, doesn't look like she can be bothered that much. She's a reluctant worker, and every ounce of her demeanour suggests she'd rather be back in her stable having a good old nosh on some hay rather than put up with some damn fool Italian jumping around on her back.

She's beautiful, though. There's a blaze of white between her eyes which drips down her nose like spilled paint, and another splash of white just broken off from the first: a mix of the shape of Africa and the way Sicily is just off the toe of Italy. She has a great depth to her – lots of heart room, lots of space for an engine, and an immensely powerful cardiovascular system. And she has big ears, just like Treve. I can tell a lot about a horse from their ears, and Enable is no different. When she's up for it, her ears are erect, almost scanning like a radar dish, taking it all in.

At Newbury in April over 10 furlongs, I ride Shutter Speed to victory, with William on Enable in third. Although Enable can't match our pace over the final three furlongs, she stays on well, which makes us think she'll be better over slightly longer distances; and even the margin of my victory is a bit deceptive, as Enable got caught in a box which hampered her a little. Two years ago I felt that Golden Horn was just that little bit higher quality than Jack Hobbs; now I feel the same way about Enable in relation to Shutter Speed.

We step Enable up in class and distance for the Cheshire Oaks, and she justifies every last bit of faith we have. The course has tight bends which can be hard to navigate for a horse with such big confident strides as hers, but she takes those bends with ease before opening up like a greyhound with three to go. She's so dominant that I can ease her down as we approach the line and still win comfortably. With Shutter Speed winning the Musidora Stakes at York, John and Prince Khalid make the decision: Shutter Speed will contest the Prix de Diane, while Enable will head for the Oaks.

This one might be something special, I think. She's like two different animals. In the mornings she's still truculent and stands her ground. I'll be asked how she was and I say, 'The usual – rubbish.' But at the races, she grows a foot like Superman. She comes alive, like a switch has been flicked. She puffs out her chest and arches her neck so the veins are sticking out in her neck, and she's chewing at the bit like a boxer going into the ring. She just knows: this is her stage.

The Oaks starts with a bang, literally: the most enormous clap of thunder as we're going up past Tattenham on the way to the start, followed by a flash of lightning and rain so torrential I can feel it drumming on my riding hat. My first priority is to settle

Enable, as it's all too easy for horses to get spooked by a storm like this. Daddys Lil Darling bolts before we even get to the stalls, with Olivier Peslier jumping clear and rolling several times on the sodden turf. Both rider and horse are unhurt, but they're scratched from the race.

I can't afford to pay them any mind: I've got my work cut out with focusing on the race ahead, riding through spray which reduces visibility, puddles which can slow even the best horse, and soaked reins starting to slip. I'll have to be extra cautious and give myself an extra yard to manoeuvre.

Ryan Moore's on the favourite Rhododendron, and it's them that I keep an eye on. For the first half of the race they're sitting right behind us. Approaching the two-furlong pole we're neck and neck, going past the early leaders and fighting it out between us with the rest nowhere. I look at Ryan's reins and they're pretty tight. *He's got the better of me*, I think, but only for a moment. We're so close that we almost touch, and for a furlong we run stride for stride. If Rhododendron's going to break us for pace it'll have to be now, because I know Enable has the stamina; but Rhododendron can't sustain her challenge. I see her start to tighten and the anxiety in Ryan's body language as he asks for what's not there. As we race past the furlong marker and the ground rises towards the finish we have daylight and I know this one's won.

I daren't take my hands off the reins to celebrate until after the line. I just have to get the job done. There'll be time for celebrations afterwards. We're all soaked through – you can see the skin of my arms where the white sleeves of my silks are plastered against them – but a win like this warms me from within. Five lengths. That's how I know she's special. Few people thought Rhododendron would get beaten, let alone by such a margin.

Amazingly, even in these conditions Enable's broken the track record. What's scary about her is not how good she is: it's how much better she's going to be.

Someone suggests that we enter her in the King George. 'Jeez, that would be bold,' John says. 'I'll have a word with her. She'll tell me what to do. Horses always tell you if you watch and listen.'

I'm being legged up onto the unraced filly Tivoli in the parade ring at Yarmouth. Out of nowhere she startles, bucking and throwing me to the ground. I hear a crack as I hit the ground, and I know it's broken. I can't lift my arm or touch my nose, but I refuse to get an X-ray as I want to ride the Prix de Diane in five days' time, when I'll be on Senga against both Rhododendron and Shutter Speed.

For that race I'm strapped to the nines and loaded up on painkillers. If we stay on the bridle I'll be fine, but I have to push Senga for about 20 seconds and the pain is excruciating, even through the painkillers. I can't even put my socks on afterwards.

The next day I go to the doctor and have an X-ray done.

'You're not going to Ascot,' he says.

Another snake on the endless snakes and ladders board that's my life. Luckily it's only a hairline fracture so I don't need an operation, but I need physio and rehab, and Enable's the dangling carrot to make me fit again.

'Three months,' says the doctor. That means six weeks, but I'll need to take another week off that if I'm to ride her in the Irish Oaks.

I'm back just in time for the Irish Oaks, and to be honest, if it wasn't Enable then I'd have waited another week or so. For her, though, anything is worth it, because she's so good and I'm not going to let anyone else ride her.

I have to ride her more or less one-handed as it hurts so much, and I go through pain barrier after pain barrier even though I'm taking painkillers like Smarties. Luckily, conditions are good: there's a tailwind and the Curragh's a wide course with tons of space, so it's almost like riding on a prairie. We're in second gear all the way round, and when I ask her to go, she flies. A quick change of gear is all that's needed. From there on in it's hands and heels, and even so we win by five and a half lengths.

On the plane home, I turn to John. 'You know when I told you we'd never find another one like Golden Horn?' I say.

He smiles. 'She's a beast, isn't she?'

Enable's groom is Imran Shahwani, who has quite a story of his own. He came from Pakistan speaking almost no English and having never ridden before. 'The boss, who is an absolute gentleman and has always looked after me, used to spend an hour teaching me to ride on ponies after third lot each day. Now I get to ride the best horse in the world.'

He starts work at 3 a.m. every day and always goes to her first, 'to brush her and give her a pick of grass and spend some time with her. She is so special, not just for me but for everyone. I won't ever have another one like her, she's a once-in-a-lifetime horse. I'm so proud to look after her and I know I'm very lucky.'

For the King George, I have to get down to my minimum weight, 8 stone 7 lb, as she's given the handicap advantage against stallions, geldings and older horses.

That means I have to lose 7lb in a week, which in turn means water and fish, nothing else. I'm right on the limit of what my body can sustain without losing my edge – I still need the strength and alertness to pilot a half-ton horse around a tricky course at high speed – but as with coming back from injury for the Irish Oaks, if I'd do it for anyone it would be Enable. No one else will ride her, not while I can stand in the irons and hold the reins.

She's 5/4 favourite, the one they're all looking out for. Since we don't want to see a sprint and we know she stays, we're confident enough to go for the simplest of plans: track the pacemaker, kick on at the top of the straight, burn them all off. That's Plan A, and that's all we need because that's just how the race unfolds.

From the moment I press the throttle, I don't see another horse. In the home straight I can hear the commentator say that I've got plenty of daylight, so I can enjoy it as we come home four and a half lengths clear. I haven't had a feeling like this since Golden Horn in the Arc two years ago. She's top drawer and that's three times she's proved it, three times that she's won by a wide margin.

As Ed Chamberlin says when signing off the ITV coverage: 'King George Day belonged to one horse. She was ready, willing, Enable.'

* * *

The Yorkshire Oaks is the same story. We have everything to lose here – she's a prohibitive favourite at 1/4 – but she's a racehorse and she needs to race. We quicken three furlongs out and I push her, but I have something left if someone comes to me. The York crowd is just about the most knowledgeable and passionate there is, and in the home straight they rise to her as one. They know. They know what they're seeing. We win by five lengths without much trouble – so little trouble, in fact, that she's looking round and idling in the last 100 metres or so, bored and wanting company. She likes to have a fight on her hands: she needs another horse to come alongside and make her go, but which horse can do that? Try to keep up with her and she'll break your lungs.

Five lengths, five-and-a-half, four-and-a-half and now another five: that's quite the record for a midsummer Group 1 programme. And an Oaks treble to boot. Not bad.

It's great prep for the Arc, where she'll have a filly's weight allowance and a favourite's chance. She's been a model of consistency and she goes on any ground. I fancy her chances.

* * *

No three-year-old filly trained in Britain or Ireland has ever won an Arc. I'm so tense before the race: I spend every day watching her, praying that she doesn't get sick or injured. The Arc's at Chantilly while Longchamp's being redeveloped, and I've got an inside draw, stall two, which means I need to be quick out of the gates to avoid being blocked. I've got 18 of the best horses in Europe and I've got to be on my wits. Chantilly can be a bit tricky at times and the rain is going to make things more complicated. If I land behind some bad horses, that can ruin my chances.

She comes off the rail so smoothly and effortlessly: it's hardly like being in an Arc at all. For a moment I toy with the idea of making the running myself, but there are some good stayers in there so I don't. Two of those stayers, Idaho and Order of St George, have me almost pinned, Idaho in front and Order of St George creeping on my quarters – but I check behind, switch back and swing outside. Job done. I'm exactly where I want her, I've got free air on my left and she's running away on the turn. Round the final bend, she's striking Order of St George's heels: that's how much power she has, to be champing at the bit even at this speed.

At York I went a bit too soon, and this is a much better field, so I don't want to take even the slightest chance of blowing it. Past the three-furlong barrier and

I count backwards from 10 in my head, like this is Cape Canaveral and I'm mission control – and the lift-off when I finally ask her to go wouldn't disgrace an actual rocket. In the blink of an eye we have four lengths, and it's all over bar the shouting – and believe me, there's plenty of that as the crowd rise in recognition that they're seeing a very special horse. I put the stick down and enjoy it, just counting down the markers. I can't believe how easy it is. That's my fifth Arc, a record for one jockey. What a way to do it, and what a horse to do it on: a destination horse, one the crowds come to see, one who puts thousands on a gate just by her presence alone. They don't come along very often.

John puts his fedora on my head afterwards. 'That race is the one I'll be watching again and again, well into my old age,' he says.

It's a surreal life, the jockey life, like still being in school. I'm in the changing room every day with kids as young as 16, and I'm getting on for 50, and we're just one big family. We don't all love each other all the time – we cross each other, we argue and all that – but overall we get on fine. We travel together, we eat together, we ride together, and when I'm in that bubble I never get old. I feel like I'm 22 when I'm with them, even though I'm the one sitting by the door of the weighing room, hanging on by my fingernails as the young ones want to kick me out. When I look at them I see myself as I was all those years ago: when they look at me they see their future, an old guy who has to wear glasses to read the form. Pat Eddery always refused to wear glasses, even when his vision got longer than his arms. 'Frankie!' he'd yell. 'Read this for me! Where am I drawn?' I used to laugh at him and call him a blind old bat – and now I'm just the same as he was then. There's always one old codger in the room, and if you can't see who it is then it's you.

It's May 2018. Enable's doing some light exercise when she suddenly shortens up. The vet says a bone spur is rubbing on her bursa, causing fluid build-up, and she'll need surgery. She's out for several months: no Coronation Cup, no King George. But John has more than one brilliant horse in his stables, so I get to ride Stradivarius in the Gold Cup.

Stradivarius is a real character, an enormous personality. As John says: 'He'd be the kind of person who went on a bus and never stopped talking. He goes out on the heath and he shouts at everyone. He particularly likes the colour blue, so he always shouts at the Godolphin string when he sees them coming. He's very nosy, he checks everything out and he's just a bundle of fun to be around. In fact, he's not unlike Frankie. I should think Frankie going into a discotheque in his youth would be rather like Stradivarius when he goes into the paddock and starts shouting and screaming at everyone.'

The Gold Cup promises to be a great contest against Vazirabad, and it delivers in spades: not just between the two of us but Torcedor as well, with all three horses finishing within a length of each other. Stradivarius is a lion and fights them all off in front of a rampant crowd. It's the best kind of racing, mental really, and I'm buzzing for hours afterwards.

I go to see Enable three or four times a week.

'Where are you going?' Catherine says.

'To the yard to see Enable.'

'Why?'

'No reason. Just to see her.'

Just to spend time with her, talk to her, bask in the warmth of her stardust.

She lives in box 32, which is itself a sign. That's my lucky number: when I go to the casino, I put my chips on 32.

I should buy shares in Nestlé to offset the cost of all the Polo mints I feed her. I spend more on Polos at the garage than I do on petrol.

'You're lucky Enable's got four legs,' John tells Catherine. So am I, or else I might not have two balls much longer.

Enable's recovery is going well, and I ride her twice a week for the month before the September Stakes. She still tricks me all the time. When I go to ride her, I put my helmet and my boots on and I can't wait to go to the stable, and I'm always thinking of the Enable of the Arc. But then we go out to work and she works bang average. She always does, and I always leave deflated. So we have to work off different signals to most other horses to know when she's ready, her own little idiosyncrasies and tells – and suddenly, with not long to go before the race, all those signals are there again.

She's 80 per cent fit, 85 per cent maximum, but that's still enough for her to see off Crystal Ocean by three and a half lengths.

And now the Arc. Treve apart, no horse has defended its title here for almost 40 years, and no horse has won the Arc with just one race all season under their belt. It's a big ask, but if any horse is up to it, it's Enable. Last year, she came off the back of a long season where she'd run six previous races; here she should be fresh from the lack of racing this time round, but she might also be undercooked. We'll see.

She's dancing in the paddock almost like it's dressage: her eyes wide open, her chest puffed up and her veins sticking out, the ultimate buzz. As we cross the course for the pre-race parade in front of the grandstand, my mouth is so dry I can't speak and my heart's leaping high in my throat. This is what I do it for: moments like this, those pure bright shining jewels of time when everything is crystallised down to its essentials.

For most of the race it's just like last year, moving freely and feeling like I have all the power in the world. At two furlongs I say to her what I always say to her, 'Come on, girl, let's go', and she responds the way she always does, with that gear change which never fails to jolt me, in the best way, deep inside. We're two lengths clear in the blink of an eye, past the furlong post, cruising to a second Arc …

… and suddenly all the strength goes out of her. The petrol gauge plummets to zero, her energy totally zapped. Sea of Class, who won the Irish and Yorkshire Oaks earlier this year, is coming from behind like a train. *Come on, girl. Half a furlong to go. Hang in there for half a furlong.* She's running through treacle, straining with everything she has, her usual fluidity gone as she tightens and strains. She's on the rivets and still Sea of Class comes. The crowd are screaming. *Come on. Do it for me.*

She dredges the depths of her soul to find that last, tiny, ebbing bit of resistance. We flash across the line almost together with Sea of Class, but I know even before the photograph that we've won. A short neck, that's all it is. Another stride, certainly another two strides, and Sea of Class would have been past. I lean down and wrap my arms round Enable's neck. She's won so many races on sheer talent, but this one she won on sheer courage and bloody-minded refusal to be beaten. 'I love you,' I say in her ear.

Paris's motto is '*Elle est battue par les flots, mais ne sombre pas*': 'She is tossed by the waves, but she does not sink'. So too for Enable, the brightest star in the City of Light.

On the way back, John tells me that she hadn't been at her best in the run-up to the race. She'd had a temperature and her blood signs had been down; and, though she'd recovered, she'd lost a bit of training time and also that last fraction of fitness. That's why she faded so badly.

'I didn't tell you because I didn't want to alter the way you rode her,' he says. 'I didn't want you to second-guess her, or yourself. I needed you to be confident. And if you hadn't gone when you did, then you'd have lost.

It was going so early which gave you the gap you needed. If you'd waited longer then Sea of Class would have run you down.'

If Enable's lack of racing almost cost her the Arc, by the same token it means that she's fresh for the Breeders' Cup at Churchill Downs. That doesn't faze me. Just another record for her to rewrite.

We're drawn near the rail in stall two, which is not where I want to be: it's rained two inches in the last 48 hours, and the firmer ground is on the outside. When she doesn't break that well and the pace is on straight away, I know we have our work cut out. I don't panic: I bide my time, find my way gradually to where I want to be, and settle in four off the fence as the early leaders come back to us. Usually I'd wait till they fade and come through between us, but I know how much of a danger Ryan is on Magical, and I can't let him get a run on me. I pull Enable back and take her round the outside of the final bend, slingshotting into the final straight as Ryan cuts the corner and comes through inside me. He's going for the line pretty early, earlier than I'd have liked, but I have to respond.

Here we go. Game on.

It's a punch-up all the way down the home straight. We get half a length on Magical and I think that might be it, but Ryan's like a wasp that won't go away. The rest are miles back as we go hammer and tongs down the middle of the course. I can't break clear, but by the same token Ryan can't close the gap. 'Racing royalty!' shrieks the commentator as we cross the line with that half-length lead still intact, and my arm thrust high and forward.

As we slow from the furious pace and begin to canter, Ryan reaches out to clasp my hand. We both know that we've been part of something special.

An Arc and Breeders' Cup double. History, right here. A few have tried, but only Enable's succeeded.

Teddy Grimthorpe, Prince Khalid's racing manager, is asked what the future holds for Enable. She's four, the age at which some horses are sent off for breeding.

'I think the most important thing is to sit back and enjoy this,' he says. 'We tend to move on far too quickly. The enormity of this, for the whole team, it's been so emotional. There's no great hurry.'

When you do my job, if you don't love horses, you might as well do something else. That's the fundamental base, to love the horse. We race, we have winners and losers, highs and lows. I've had special horses over the years, such as Dubai Millennium and Golden Horn. I thought I'd never have another like Golden Horn, and I was wrong. But when I think I'll never have another like Enable, I know I'm right. She's just that little bit more. She takes me to places, emotional places, that other horses can't.

She's become a household name: the horse that everybody wants to come and see, which in itself creates pressure and a feeling of responsibility. There are a whole lot of people involved in getting Enable to the start line in as good a shape as she can be – John, Imran, the other stables staff – but once we leave the paddock and head up to the race itself it's just me and her. That bond is special because I can feel it, I can smell it, and it's all made much sharper and deeper by the love of the crowd, and again the bond is deepened. Every time she sets foot on the racecourse is just amazing. I can touch the warmth, the pressure, the excitement of everyone. I love it, and so does she.

In 2019 I win the Gold Cup on Stradivarius for a second time, and give the bookies a hell of a fright along the way – not for the Gold Cup itself, at which we were evens, but because I've also won the first three races before that too, and for the bookies the spectre of 28 September 1996 is never far away. There's already a statue of me near the entrance to the Royal Enclosure, and for a few hours it looks like they might need to commission another one. But I lose out in the fifth on Turgenev despite leading with a furlong left, and the streak is over. Twenty years ago I might have won that – he begins as favourite having been 16/1 earlier, the price slashed by the sheer weight of money going on us – and he gives me a great spin, but it's not to be. Four on Ladies' Day is a good day in anyone's book, so I'm not going to cry.

The bookies are changing the way they let people bet on me. Skybet and bet365 have restricted the number of my horses that can be permed together, Coral accepts accumulators only with the final two runners being paid at starting prices rather than the morning odds, and other firms have limited stakes. People put accumulators on me the way they don't on other jockeys. I'd love to be able to make their dreams come true.

Enable's not getting any keener to train now she's five. It takes her longer to get ready, she can be truculent, and we have to mix things up a bit to keep her interested: work her on the racecourse, give her company, put her in front, let her trail. If you go into her box she lets you know that it's her space and not yours, and if you mess around in there when she's not in the mood, she'll split you in two. Some mornings it takes an hour to catch her.

She's doing everything perfectly competently, but the hunger's not there. She's going through the motions, not concentrating – then suddenly she's quicker, fitter, sharper, in the zone. The edge is back.

We run in the Eclipse Stakes at Sandown. It's a 10-furlong race and she's a 12-furlong horse, so I have to be careful not to be outkicked at the end by a faster finisher. I keep her up near the lead right from the start, and when I turn for home she grabs the bit – I'm the last one off the bridle: all the others are already straining – and wants to go. I have to make her wait till the two pole, and it takes everything I have to hold her back. It's not just her size, scope, stride and the amount of gears she has: it's her insane will to win.

Again Magical runs us close, just as she did at Churchill Downs last autumn, but again we have enough to hold her off. Three-quarters of a length, exactly the same margin as in that Breeders' Cup. The Eclipse has been going since 1886, and Enable's only the third mare to win. I'm as ecstatic as when I won my first race on her, and with the Eclipse on it now, her CV is unbelievable. She's very special.

'Ohhhhhhh, Frankie Dettori,' the crowd sing, to the tune of The White Stripes' 'Seven Nation Army'. That was the song the Italian football fans sang when we won the World Cup in 2006. Now it belongs to another Italian too.

The King George is a vintage field. I'm drawn widest of all in stall 11, which forces me wide for the first three furlongs. I can't afford to go five wide all the way, but no one will let me in. I have to drop back to get closer to the rail, conceding ground to Crystal Ocean and James Doyle. Eventually I find myself behind Waldgeist, but the horse I've got to beat is Crystal Ocean.

Past four to go and I'm thinking Waldgeist will wait, so I do likewise.

Three out and I make a move onto Crystal Ocean's flank.

Two out and I ask Enable for the works.

She leaps forward. Crystal Ocean fights back on my inside, holding his ground. Crystal Ocean gets a nose in front. Enable comes back level. James Doyle's silks are like a black shadow which I can't shake. On the commentary, Simon Holt's voice is cracking as he screams, 'Crystal Ocean will not give in!'

The battles with Magical were one thing, but this is another level: compelling, unrelenting, a battle royal in front of the grandstand, a stretch run like no other. It's a men's final at Wimbledon, 12-all in the final set; it's a heavyweight title fight deep into the later rounds; it's Grundy and Bustino in the same race 44 years ago, the one they call 'Race of the Century'. It's the hardest-fought race of my career. The world fades away to just us: Enable against Crystal Ocean, me against James. Head to head, toe to toe, neither prepared to give an inch. It's racing at its purest, world-class performers on the ragged edge of their limits and beyond.

With half a furlong left I get a neck, and I cling to that gap for all I'm worth. I'm crouched flat to Enable's withers as we cross the line, and again I know it's ours without needing the photo; but Crystal Ocean has lost nothing except first place.

Imran comes to lead Enable back to the winner's enclosure. I reach down and hug him. So many people love Enable, but there are three of us who know her that little bit better than everyone else: John, Imran and me. Trainer, groom and jockey. We know her that little bit better, and we love her that little bit more. And she never stops making our jaws drop with her ability and courage. A horse for the ages has won a race for the ages. These are the moments I'll remember when I'm in my rocking chair and my grandchildren don't want to hear the same old story for the 57th time.

I'm totally drained by the emotion and intensity of the race. When I come back from doing my interviews,

I see Sir Michael Stoute, Crystal Ocean's trainer, waiting for me outside the weighing room. He doesn't say much: just puts his hand on my shoulder, a simple, heartfelt gesture which I very much appreciate.

The public will probably only see Enable two more times, at York and the Arc, so I want them to enjoy her, because like all horses she'll be a long time retired. Although I have a pretty healthy ego and have never been accused of being knowingly understated, I know that when we're in union she's the star, not me.

The Yorkshire Oaks is scheduled to be Enable's penultimate race. She beats Magical easily, but the race is less memorable than the occasion: it's the last time Enable's due to appear in England, with 'Go Enable!' flags being handed out to racegoers. I'm in tears. It's not quite the end of the affair, but it's getting closer every day.

Newmarket runs an open weekend every September, where members of the public can come and see behind the scenes at the stables and watch horses galloping on the heath. No prizes for guessing who's star of the show. They come to see her in their thousands and from all over the world, because she's so well-travelled. She's won Group 1s in England, Ireland, France and America;

in fact, since the 2017 Arc was at Chantilly, this year's King George was the first time she'd ever won twice on the same track.

She's not the greatest racehorse of my lifetime: that's Frankel. She's not the greatest racehorse ever owned by Prince Khalid, because that was Frankel too. At the moment she's not even the best in John's stables: Cracksman is ranked first in the world, with Enable joint eighth. But none of that matters. Frankel made it look all too easy because for him it was. Enable's done it the easy way and the hard way. Her talent came through in the vast winning margins of her 2017 season; her attitude has won her all those tight victories of the last year or so. She loves the crowds, she loves the racing, she loves the challenge. I remember how bored she was at her first Yorkshire Oaks, looking round as she cruised to victory. People love her because she gives of herself.

No horse has ever won three Arcs in a row, and only one jockey has – Pat Eddery, on three different horses between 1985 and 1987. Only Treve has even attempted the treble before. I'd be lying if I said I wasn't nervous. Of course I'm nervous. I get nervous from the night before onwards, and I get quite obnoxious, so my family kind of run away from me. But it's part and parcel of riding the favourite in the Arc.

The field is stacked: Japan won the International Stakes at York, Sottsass won the French Derby, Magical's in there, as is Ghaiyyath, who won a recent Group 1 race in Germany by 14 lengths. I've got the expectation of the world on my shoulders, which is great. I'd rather be in that position than not, so I will try to enjoy it. I'm not physically as good as I was at 25, but what I've lost there I've gained in experience, and I know experience will be crucial in a race like this.

John and I walk the course beforehand. John presses his stick into the ground to see how much give there is. It goes in a long way. Soft ground from all the rain lately. Enable likes it when it's good to firm: she spins her wheels on soft ground.

John and I look at each other: Houston, we have a problem.

In the parade before the race, we're introduced to the crowd. When the commentator says, 'Et maintenant, numero huit, le champion Enable,' the roar from the crowd breaks over my head like a waterfall.

I must ride the race as it is, not how I'd like it to be. The early pace is hot and I have to stay in touch. Enable's feeling good as we come into the home straight, but her stamina and speed aren't quite as stratospheric as they used to be, especially on this ground, and I want to wait as long as I dare before unleashing her. Two out and Sottsass comes alongside. Go now or hold back? These are split-second decisions, and you never know how they'll play out. If you win, you were right; if you lose, you were wrong. The binary purity of sport.

Go, I think. *Go now.*

For the 13th race in a row I ask Enable for the turbo boost, and for the 13th race in a row she gives it to me, but it's not quite the same as it was. I'm clear at the furlong post, and even with 100 left I'm still in front, but she's not moving quite the way she can, and if someone comes past us now we have no response.

Someone does come past us. It's Waldgeist, sweeping through so magnificently that even though he only gets to us with 50 to go he's almost two lengths clear by the post. We've beaten him three times before, twice last year in the Arc and the Breeders' Cup and once this year in the King George, but the only race that matters today is this one, and he's done us good and proper.

The air goes out of the crowd as we cross the line in second: a mass deflation, a giant balloon popped. Twelve wins in a row for us, and now this. Unlucky 13th indeed. But what could I do? With the going as it was, I could see the sucker punch coming. Maybe I should have waited longer, and if I had then we might have won it, but we might also have lost by more. If the going had been good to soft, we'd almost certainly have won it. If, if, if. If my auntie had bollocks she'd be my uncle. There are no excuses. You ride the conditions – that's what makes racing the sport it is – and today Waldgeist rode them better than we did. That's all there is to it.

You don't win 'em all. I certainly don't love her any the less for losing, and I've never worried about being beaten on her. She was beaten in her second race out – by me, ironically enough, on Shutter Speed. An unbeaten record can be a burden. It's not the be-all and end-all. Some horses stir you at a level way beyond and below the statistics, and she's one of those. Boy, is she one of those.

Most people assume that Enable will be retired to breed, but Prince Khalid has other ideas. No, he says, let's give her another season. It would be the easiest thing in the world for him to put her out to stud, and it would make perfect commercial sense. But Prince Khalid is a horse-man as much as he's a businessman, and he thinks not only that Enable still has another season left in her but also that she, and we, should go out there and enjoy it.

'I think Prince Khalid really enjoys seeing her race, and the filly loves training and loves racing,' John says. 'She hasn't been over-raced in her career: just one run as a two-year-old and then she was busy but loving her racing at three. Then of course we had an interruption with an injury and a little surgery at four, so she only had three runs, and then last year she had four runs. I know we think six is old, but actually in the world of jump racing they are just coming to their prime at that age, and I've always felt down the years that if they are happy and enjoying their racing they are probably at their zenith at five anyhow. It was always the opinion of the great old American trainers like Charlie Whittingham and Woody Stephens, and to that extent I'm a great believer in it. It's not like she's been having 10 races a year: she's only had seven races in the last two years.'

I know there's going to be an end to it one day. She can't go on for ever. With every other horse, even the best ones, I've always been able to accept that they'll go to stud sooner or later, but with Enable, even the prospect is awful. I want to pause time so I can hold her here where she is, frozen for ever. I try to cherish every moment. I feel like I'm living with someone who's going to pass away, and if that sounds melodramatic then fine, but that's genuinely how I feel. Everyone wants to know what I think, and each time they ask me it cuts at me and opens up the wound again.

But right now I've got one more year with my special girl, this one who's touched my heart like no other. I'm so thrilled I can hardly speak.

* * *

And then, of course, Covid happens. Everything's locked down, racing's suspended, I'm hardly even allowed to go out and exercise. It's the longest I've been at home in God knows how long, and I hate being cooped up.

Racing resumes just in time for me not to be carted off to the loony bin, but it's not the same without crowds. Enable's not the same either. Her metabolism's changing, and she's carrying a bit more weight than usual. I need to nurse her through this season. Last season I thought was my last with her. This one definitely will be, so I have to make the days count, each and every one. It's like taking a small mouthful and enjoying the taste more, because there's not much left.

She finishes second to Ghaiyyath at the Eclipse, and when I know we're beaten, I ease down to save her for what's to come.

At the King George there are only three of us in the race: Japan, Sovereign and us. Sovereign sets the pace in driving rain while Japan settles in at the back, leaving us to be the filling in the sandwich. With two to go I move up alongside Sovereign. I can't hear a lot from behind me, so I think that Japan's either doing some stealth sneaking or that I've got a bit of daylight. I take a look back, and see he's in trouble. All we have to do is find another gear, and that's what we do. When we cross the line first I scream 'I love you!', and my voice echoes round and round the empty stands.

Enable's the first horse to win three King Georges, and it's my seventh. I remember the Queen telling me when I'd won four that Lester won seven. Well, now I've equalled him, and I'd like to remind her! But of course the pandemic means Her Majesty's not here.

Even though Enable's not getting better, her enthusiasm throughout the race today was plain to see, and she's still thriving with racing. When she was a three-year-old she had complete disregard for any and all opposition, plus the weight allowance from the older horses. It's different now. She's more like Muhammad Ali in his later years, relying on guile and experience rather than sheer speed and reflexes. A six-year-old mare is different to a three-year-old filly. She's robust, wiser, tougher. John likens her to the great tennis players who get to the fifth set and use their mental strength to win it above anything else.

The dream is the third Arc. We came so close last year, and with this kind of performance we're still in with a shot.

She's 1/14 for the September Stakes, a last warm-up for the Arc. It's an emphatic seven-length victory: a nice blow and a good day out, a race which will have

brought her on nicely, more mental than physical preparation. But it was a weak field, and her wow factor has
gone. Last year I *thought* she'd win the Arc, and if it
had been better going underfoot I still think she would
have. This time I *hope* she wins. There's a difference,
and I know it all too well. It's not impossible, but it will
involve all the cards falling our way.

The dream is still alive, though, and that's all that
matters. I want her to be remembered for ever.

Covid rules mean we'll need to spend a fortnight in
quarantine when we get back from the Arc, but none of
us care. Teddy says he'd have swum here if necessary.

The ground for the Arc is wet, just as it was last year,
and I can feel our chances slipping away even before we
get to the start. Persian King takes the lead and sets the
pace, but it's too slow and the ground's too soft. When
I press the button two furlongs out, there's nothing.
Three years ago she was untouchable here. Two years
ago she faded but held on. Last year she faded and lost.
Now she doesn't even have anything to fade from. I
can't pick her up, not even using the whip. Her time has
come and her time has gone.

She finishes sixth. It's the first time in her career she's
not been placed. Nineteen races: 15 wins, two seconds,
a third and this. That's it. All over, and in front of an

empty grandstand to boot. This is how it ends, not with a bang but with a whimper. This is not how it should have ended. She deserved a final victory in front of a rapturous crowd cheering her home to the last echo.

I get off and cuddle her. There's no horse who can replace what we did together. We've had an unbelievable journey, and I'm very grateful for that.

Enable's road is run, and though mine isn't yet I know that one day it will be. I'm not going to race for ever either. The sands are running through my hourglass the same way they've run through hers, and I know that part of my wanting to stall the end of her time is wanting to stall my own too.

I dread the day I have to stop. Nothing will replace what I've got. I've woken up every morning for 35 years doing exactly the same thing, going out there, competing, travelling the world, all the ups and downs, people adoring me and hating me. All of that, and one day – bang! All gone. But it has to end sometime. Exactly when that will be, I don't know. I won't do it when I get to a certain number – 55, 60, whatever. I'll do it when it feels right, and that'll be when I'm no longer competitive or no longer enjoying it. Perhaps when I have to slide off rather than do the flying dismount. But already I'm a slave to that. If I don't do it, I get booed. I see mothers from a mile off dragging their poor kids, saying, 'Come on, he's going to jump.' I think, *God, I've got no choice.*

I'm a little kid from Italy. I've been places, seen things and met people you wouldn't dream of. Sheikhs, kings, queens, famous people. So I can't eat a chocolate cake. That's no price. And sometimes I do eat it anyway and I just put up with the consequences. But most of all I do what I do because I love to ride. I go out there, I get on my horse and everybody is shouting my name. That doesn't happen to other riders. I love it. I love it. I love it.

I'm loyal to people. I've been with Pete for 30 years, even though someone tries to steal me from him at least once a year. Big agencies, hotshot agents, all dangling promises of this and that in front of me. I tell them all to get stuffed. He's my agent, he's my friend, I trust him with my life. You can't put a price on that.

My life follows the seasons. Over Christmas and New Year, I'm with my family, often skiing with the children. When they go back to school, I lose the weight I've put on over Christmas and prepare for the Middle East circuit: Bahrain, Qatar and Saudi Arabia, two or three months till the season resumes in England at the end of March. The years go quicker and quicker. I don't have much time for getting bored. My life is like putting a treadmill as fast as it can go and jumping on it: and I'm on it at the moment, going a million miles an hour. I've been in the fast lane for so long that I've become addicted to it. But nothing lasts for ever. Once I stop all this madness, when I step off that treadmill, I'll just have to readjust: reset myself, reset the treadmill at a different pace. Start another life. God, it will be hard. And scary, too. But I'll find a way.

It's Enable's last day at Clarehaven before going off to stud. She has her picture taken in Prince Abdullah's colours, the lovely pink, green and white she's worn so well. The entire stable staff come out into the front yard, and I take her on three laps, each one to a standing ovation. It feels like death, but it's also a reminder of life, of why we do this job.

She knows she's loved. That's important to me. And she also knows she's going. I can feel she does. This is her saying goodbye to all of us just as we're saying goodbye to her. She's going to the breeding shed and not the slaughterhouse, but still: this phase of her life is over. I can go and see her when she has a baby. Maybe I'll ride one of her kids. She'll be mated with Kingman, so those are some pretty decent horse genes right there.

I can hardly see through my tears. Everyone else is crying too, and I mean everyone. This is what a horse like Enable can do: this is how she can touch your soul. When I go home from here I'm going to cry for two days straight, like a teenager who's just broken up with his first love. I take a little piece of her tail, a scissor snip she doesn't even notice but which will mean the world to me, which will remind me of the way her tail would stream out horizontal behind her when she was in full flight.

I think of how often I've been at one with her: anatomically, mechanically, mentally. It's not simply how many races we won, though God knows there've been enough, and the most prestigious ones too: three King Georges, two Arcs, a Breeders' Cup. Nor was it the way we won them, usually by lengths but now and then by inches, for we could both grit it out on the days when everything didn't come easy and shiny.

No, it's simpler than that. Like any two beings who are properly in love, we understood each other perfectly, and we brought out the best in each other. As distraught as I am that our partnership is over, I'm more thankful to have had it at all. That partnership wasn't just the races and the adulation. It was all the times I'd go over to the stables just to see her and give her Polo mints, it was the simple joy we'd take in each other's company, and it was the dawn training gallops on the Limekilns above Newmarket: the sun coming up, plumes of breath billowing in frigid air, empty expanses of heath all around, and me and my girl arrowing across the turf in perfect harmony, flying, flying, flying.

PICTURE CREDITS

SECTION II

Page 1: Courtesy of the author

Page 2, top: Mike Hewitt/Allsport/Getty Images

Page 2, bottom: Julian Herbert/Getty Images

Page 3, top: Courtesy of the author

Page 3, bottom: © Jonathan Brady/PA Archive/PA Images/Alamy Stock Photo

Page 4, top: Jean Catuffe/Getty Images

Page 4, bottom: © Julian Herbert/PA Archive/PA Images/Alamy Stock Photo

Page 5, top: Courtesy of the author

Page 5, bottom: Steve Parsons/PA Archive/PA Images/Alamy Stock Photo

Page 6, top: Lo Chun Kit/Getty Images

Page 6, bottom: Eric Patterson/CSM/Sipa USA/PA Images/Alamy Stock Photo

Page 7, top left: Eóin Noonan/Sportsfile via Getty Images

Page 7, top right: Courtesy of the author

Page 7, bottom: Courtesy of the author

Page 8, top: Foto via www.imago-images.de/Imago/PA Images

Page 8, bottom: Alan Crowhurst/Getty Images

ACKNOWLEDGEMENTS

To everyone who has helped and supported me throughout this wonderful life and career. You all know who you are. Thank you to Boris Starling for putting it all into words.